SEED TO
VISION

How GOD-Inspired Ideas
Become REALITY

"If you have dreams and plans that you would one day like to see become a reality, then Steve Finn's new book *Seed to Vision* is a must-read for you. God gave him a vision, and when he put his hands to the plow he never looked back. This book will equip you with eight practical tools to help you accomplish your goals as you pursue God's call on your life."

—Jim McBride, executive pastor, Sherwood Baptist Church and executive producer, Sherwood Pictures

"I'm grateful that Steve Finn followed God's call and began Chestnut Mountain Ranch back in 2006. In this book, Steve outlines the tools that helped him launch out in obedience—tools that will encourage and help you as you respond to what God has called you to do."

—J. Frank Harrison III, chairman and CEO, Coca-Cola Bottling Co. Consolidated

"Steve Finn has written a brilliant story, his story, of how God can plant a seed and deliver a dream. *Seed to Vision* is a must-read for leaders who want their God-sized dreams to be realized. This book offers both inspiration and practical principles to help you achieve your most meaningful pursuits in life."

—Dan Reiland, executive pastor, 12Stone Church
Atlanta, Georgia

"This book will enlighten you as to how much God can accomplish through you if you are brave enough to follow the path He created you to follow and trust Him along that path."

—Paul Smith, former president, Kroger
Atlanta market

"I've known Steve Finn for more than 15 years and have been privileged to see his vision to change children's lives and restore families in West Virginia become a reality. The tools Steve offers to those who want to realize their own dreams have been proven through his experiences and the lessons he learned along the way."

—Eddie Staub, founder and executive director, Eagle Ranch

"I have known Steve Finn for close to 20 years. He always exudes faith in God, in his mission, and in his personal purpose, and he is a 'fisher of folks' into that faith. As life moves forward we all have seen bad things happen, and we always strive to improve circumstances for ourselves and those we love. Rarely do we know those who intentionally agree to sacrifice their own and their family's comforts in order to improve the lives of others—to change young boys with a life of little or no potential to young men who possess the promise, knowledge, skills, and self confidence needed to make a good life and perhaps share those messages and joys on to the next generation. Steve and his story are a true inspiration for all of us to follow to play a part in creating a better world."

—Nancy C. Panoz, cofounder, Chateau Elan Hotel and Resort, founder and CEO, Conan LLC

SEED TO
VISION

How GOD-Inspired Ideas
Become REALITY

STEPHEN P. FINN *with* TREY DUNHAM

NEW HOPE
PUBLISHERS
Gospel-Centered. Missions-Driven.

Birmingham, Alabama

New Hope® Publishers
PO Box 12065
Birmingham, AL 35202-2065
NewHopePublishers.com
New Hope Publishers is a division of WMU®.

Names: Finn, Steve, 1969- author.
Title: Seed to vision : how God-inspired ideas become reality
    by Steve Finn with Trey Dunham.
Description: First [edition].
Birmingham : New Hope Publishers, 2017.
Includes bibliographical references.
Identifiers: LCCN 2017010135 | ISBN 9781625915214 (permabind)
Subjects: LCSH: Dreams—Religious aspects—Christianity.
Success—Religious aspects—Christianity.
Classification: LCC BR115.D74 F56 2017 | DDC 248.2—dc23
LC record available at https://lccn.loc.gov/2017010135

ISBN-13: 978-1-62591-521-4

N174119 • 0517 • 2.5M1

Do your best to present yourself to God as one approved, a worker who does not need to be ashamed and who correctly handles the word of truth.

—2 Timothy 2:15

CONTENTS

ACKNOWLEDGMENTS

God has used people to shape people throughout the Scriptures. It is no different for me. I want to acknowledge my father, Russell Finn, for showing me how to stay focused on Christ through sickness and up until his death. My father was a seed planter in my life. My mother, Joyce, for praying over me throughout my life, and speaking encouragement to pursue Christ always. My wife, Dawn, for being my "armor bearer." Dawn is my chief counsel, my prayer partner, and my wingman.

I want to thank all the men and women who helped shape me. God used you at seasons in my life to refine me, encourage me, and redirect me. The ministry of Chestnut Mountain Ranch is here because God used you to shape me.

I want to thank some key organizations that impacted me along this journey . . . the men and women of Gwinnett County Police in Atlanta, Georgia. I want to thank Eddie Staub and the staff of Eagle Ranch Children's Home in Georgia. I want to thank the ministry staff of 12Stone Church for pouring your time and resources into my life and Chestnut Mountain Ranch. I want to thank Brody Holloway and the ministry staff of Snowbird Wilderness Outfitters in North Carolina.

Above all, God gave me life, has sustained me through the years, and will always be my sole Provider. Thanks be to God!

Steve Finn
Morgantown, West Virginia
2016

INTRODUCTION

She stared at me from underneath a wild shock of bright red hair, but it wasn't a defiant stare. It was the stare of someone deep in thought, considering what they were just hearing as if it were a new and unique idea. I repeated across the cluttered kitchen table, "You have a choice to make, and for you, I think it could mean life or death."

Her mother sat next to her. Same fiery red hair but dulled with wisps of gray. She looked tired, worn. They both did. The girl was maybe 16 years old. She slouched a bit in her chair but continued to stare at me from under her bangs. She didn't say anything.

At the time I was a police officer with the Gwinnett County Police Department in the metropolitan Atlanta area, and we had been following up on some leads regarding an armed robbery. This part of the city was well known for its gangs, and serious, violent crimes were not unusual.

I stared back, wondering what thoughts were going through her head, what things she had experienced growing up in such a tough environment. She seemed older than 16; her eyes seemed to belie someone with more life and street experience than most of us would get in a lifetime. She had seen some rough stuff, been around the wrong people. It showed.

"I know that you know what happened with this robbery," I said quietly and calmly. "I know you know something, and right now you're trying to decide if you should tell me or keep quiet." I paused and let those words sink in. I wanted her to know I knew what was going on in her mind. I hoped it would help take down her guard.

She didn't move or react except to look down at the table. Fifteen then thirty seconds passed in silence; her mother and I waited for her to respond.

Finally, after two full minutes her mom offered, "She's mixed up with some bad people. She's running around with some gang-bangers. I really don't know what to do, but I am worried about her."

I didn't say anything in response, only nodded ever so slightly, keeping my eyes on her. Her red hair glistened in the fluorescent light. Its hum filled the room. I fidgeted with my pencil, tapping at the open notebook on the table, hoping she would give me some-thing—a name, an address, a phone number I could follow. Instead, she continued to stare at the table with eyes that said, "I just don't know what to do."

Her lip quivered slightly, but she did not move or raise her eyes.

"You can do the right thing here. You can tell me what happened. I am just afraid that if you keep going down this path, making bad choices, you will either end up dead or in jail. And I don't want either of those things for you."

She took a long, deep breath and slowly exhaled but said nothing. She closed her eyes, held them tight for two seconds, then slowly opened them and resumed her focus on the table in front of her. I waited, hoping she would break the silence. But she held; some-thing held it back in her. The hum from the lights seemed to grow louder. Neither of us moved for a very long time. A car, blaring loud music, passed by outside.

"Well, here's my card," I said finally after ten minutes of silence. "Call me if you want to talk." I stood up slowly, the chair grinding and whining against the tile of the kitchen floor. I continued, "I hope you will call me. I hope you will do the right thing here. I want something better for you than this kind of life."

I turned to her mother and shrugged my shoulders slightly, smiled, and thanked her for her cooperation. She said she would call if her daughter wanted to talk.

I left the house with a feeling of dread. Part of me knew there was only so much I could do for that young woman and another that wanted to run back, grab her by the shoulders, and shake her until she understood how dire her situation was. She needed another voice in her life, one that would point her toward a new and better and safer life. She needed someone to introduce her to Jesus, to help her understand His love for her and His desire that she would have a joyful, full, and abundant life. I felt a slight wave of anxiety wash over me, knowing I might never see her again, or when I did it might be too late.

I pulled my car door closed with a little more force than normal. I looked over the steering wheel into the night, wondering what else I could have done for this red-haired girl.

Four days later my partner and I were in a nearby neighborhood in a fake taxi, monitoring activity at a known neighborhood gang house. It had been a long day, and not much was happening. I struggled at moments to keep my eyes open. Stakeouts are not as glamorous as you might think.

I was jerked back to full attention as a call came over the radio. It was an automobile accident with fatalities. We listened for the location and realized we were just a couple blocks from the scene. We decided we should go take a look and called in our response.

We were the first officers on the scene. It was not pretty. A late-model Lincoln had collided head-on with a Jeep. Smoke mixed with steam from the engines filled the air. The street was strewn with twisted metal and shattered glass.

The Lincoln had struck with such force that the body of the Jeep had been shorn off the frame and lay to the side. Half stuck through the window was the driver. He was not moving. I looked inside the

Lincoln and saw its driver in a crumpled heap across the front seat. Blood oozed from a gash in his forehead. He wasn't moving, but I could see familiar tattoos on his forearm and back. Gang signs. He was still too.

I turned to return to our car and alert dispatch to details of the scene. We would need multiple ambulances. As I walked, the first fire truck arrived and two firefighters jumped out. I pointed them to the two victims and continued to the car.

"We have another body here," the firefighter who had gone to the Lincoln yelled. I turned just as he pulled out the driver, his body broken and covered in blood. He set him carefully on the pavement then turned to look in the car.

There are moments when you know something before it happens, before you see it with your own eyes, and for some reason I knew who I was going to find in that car. My heart sank. I felt sick to my stomach. Still, I walked over only to confirm what I already knew. I peered over the door and into the front seat. Crumpled into the passenger foot well was a mop of red hair. I turned and walked away—it was her.

Over the years, I have thought of that day many times, wondering if there was any way, anything I could have done to save that young girl. I don't know. I believe in a sovereign God, One who is in control of everything, and I don't think her life was ever outside of His control or purpose for her.

But the experience shaped me, changed and awakened something in me. I was seeing kid after kid make choices that would lead them to destructive lives, lives full of pain and hate, and I wanted to do something to help, to somehow step into that world and make a difference.

I was too late for the red-haired girl, but I knew there were others I could help, others who needed me to do something. I had no idea what, but that on day and many others like it, I knew I had to try.

Maybe you have a similar stirring in your heart—a desire to do something to make the world a better place—but don't know where to start or how to begin. That was me, and somehow, by the grace of God and through His miraculous leading, I started to discover abilities and talents and opportunities to begin working with troubled kids, to start to make a difference in their lives.

This book is my story, the path God laid out for me. Hopefully it will also be an encouragement to you to follow God's leading in your life and begin to develop and hone the necessary skills and abilities you will need to change your world and the lives of people around you.

My father loved kids, and he loved his home state, West Virginia. He was a great dad who taught me about life and God and values. He loved my friends who would come over; he'd teach us about cars and guns and how to make a campfire. I couldn't imagine a better man for a father.

But, for some reason, God decided his time on earth would be short. He died from cancer when I was 13. It was one of the worst times of my life because I loved him so much, and he loved me.

After his death, my mom and I relocated to Georgia. So I lost not only my father but also all my familiar surroundings. It probably isn't surprising that I started to go a little off the rails through my teen years. My mom did her best. But it was a lot to expect, and I ran wild.

However, as these things go, God got ahold of me again in college, and I started to change. Then, almost out of nowhere, I started thinking about my dad and his love for kids and his home state. I started to remember how he would come into my room at night, and we would talk about starting a home for troubled kids in West Virginia because he saw the need was as great then as it is today. In 2016 CNN reported 27 heroin overdoses in a four-hour period in Huntington, West Virginia. And then there is the fact that 50 percent of babies born in Harrison County, West Virginia, are born to mothers who used drugs, alcohol, cigarettes, or caffeine, with half of those babies needing treatment for withdrawal symptoms. This drug epidemic plays into dropout rates, unemployment rates, and hopelessness. In a state health report by the United Health Foundation that ranks states by analyzing areas such as rising rates of drug deaths, obesity, diabetes, and children in poverty, West Virginia was in the 47th slot.

I DON'T KNOW HOW, BUT THAT SEED STARTED TO GROW IN ME.

I don't know how, but that seed started to grow in me. God was directing my family's life to a greater calling, and after 12 years of law enforcement, God was moving the vision forward. This vision would later become known as Chestnut Mountain Ranch.

To be honest, I was scared to death. I didn't know anything about anything and certainly didn't feel like I was ready to launch a ministry. But over time, and with lots of help from people God placed in my life, I started to gain some skills and tools I would need for my mission. I didn't have an MBA, and I wasn't a skilled carpenter. What I gained weren't ordinary tools. These were spiritual tools, and little did I know how vital they would be as we packed up and headed north to the mountains of Appalachia.

I decided to write this book because I often run into people who have a stirring they believe to be from God, and they just do not know where to begin. They feel inadequate and unskilled—just like I did—and they reach out to get some help, some counsel, and some guidance. And I share what I have now put in this book.

God needs to develop some skills in us, and we need to work on refining our ability to use them. And when we work in concert with Him, we truly can change the world.

As I have gone through the process of envisioning, starting, and then trying to grow Chestnut Mountain Ranch, I have found that certain themes keep coming up in my life—tools, if you will, that I have found myself picking up over and over. Tools I believe make all the difference in the success of the ministry God has entrusted to us.

Anyone who wants to build something needs tools, and I believe this is especially true for anyone who wants to build something for God. We cannot go into the world and get to work unless we have some skills and abilities at our disposal. I couldn't do that as a police officer, and I could not do it with Chestnut Mountain Ranch. I don't think you will be able to do it either.

ANYONE WHO WANTS TO BUILD SOMETHING NEEDS TOOLS, AND I BELIEVE THIS IS ESPECIALLY TRUE FOR ANYONE WHO WANTS TO BUILD SOMETHING FOR GOD.

The great thing is that God provides what we need, and every tool I have in my toolbox is something He developed in me. When I was a kid, my father taught me how to hold a hammer and properly use a saw. My mother taught me how to hold a pencil and load the dishwasher. God teaches and trains us to become skillful in using the tools we need to accomplish His will for us.

These are the tools God used and helped me to become proficient at using, and I think He will train you to use them in your life as well.

I don't want to give the impression that this is an exhaustive list of all the tools you will need to launch into what God has called you to do. But I do find that I go back to these tools time and time again, dust them off, sharpen them, and put them to work. And I firmly believe God has given us these tools to help us do great things, to help us change the world, for His glory and His renown.

TOOL NO. 1:
A SEED

Steve, are you awake?"

The door creaked a bit, and a narrow shaft of light from the hallway cut through the dark of the room.

"Yeah, Dad," I said, "I'm awake." I rubbed my eyes, trying to adjust to the light that now flooded into my room as he opened the door even wider. He stood still for a second, his silhouette frozen like a statue. I could hear him breathing. Between each breath I could hear the faint hum of the fish tank filter.

"Can't sleep?" I asked as he gathered himself and placed one foot, then another, into my room. I was 12 years old.

He shuffled slowly across the carpet, "Yeah, this medication keeps me up."

It wasn't unusual for my dad to come into my room in the middle of the night. For two years he had been sick, and he had trouble sleeping. His body was thinning. He could no longer move with the same agility I remembered from a few years earlier. As hard as he tried, he was starting to lose the fight.

My father was a hardworking man with big dreams. The first one in his family to go to college, he earned two degrees. He told me that if I didn't want to end up spending my life digging ditches somewhere, then I should get a good education and work hard in school.

He believed that men should be men—they should work hard and protect their families. My father was my hero. I thought he was invincible.

And then cancer entered our lives.

From age 11 to 13, I saw the illness slowly overcoming my hero. It became more and more difficult for him to walk. He lost most of his weight and was reduced physically to a shadow of his former self.

While the cancer whittled away at his body, my father started to grow in other ways. Maybe because he knew the end was coming, maybe because it took weakness to awaken him—for whatever the reason, it was during that time that I saw his focus shift from money and retirement to spiritual things. It was during his fight with cancer that he strove to get as close to God as he could.

And it was during those two years that he would come into my room in the early morning hours. He said the light in my fish tank would fill him with a sense of peace. He enjoyed the way the fish moved and floated in the invisible currents of the glass aquarium, the way the light reflected off the walls: blue and green and aqua bouncing off the ceiling.

Many nights we would stare together at the water. Neither of us would say a word, but would simply enjoy the moment, the quiet of the night enveloping us. Sometimes he would sit at the end of my bed, I'd prop myself up under a pillow, and we would just look at that tank for hours before one of us would speak.

He'd tell me how he always wanted a better life for me and my sisters, and how he'd been so thankful for us. He told me he was thankful to be part of a family, for my mom, my sisters, for the good life we had had together.

"Not everyone gets to have a family, son," he told me one night. "Not everyone is as lucky as us."

I'd stare into the tank. I had two goldfish, and they liked to hide in a small castle wedged into the blue rocks piled up in the far corner. Side by side, they guarded the castle door, eyes darting quickly as if looking for intruders.

One night when he came in, we talked for a while about what happened at school that day. He asked about my science test, what had happened at recess, what I thought of my teachers. After about 30 minutes, he got really quiet. I could tell he was thinking about something. I waited.

"Steve," he said quietly. I strained to hear because I knew what he was about to say was important. "Someday, when I get better, when we beat this cancer, we're going to move back to the mountains of West Virginia, and we're going to open a place for boys—for boys that don't have good families, for boys that don't have good dads."

I didn't say anything. The words seemed to bounce around the room, mixing and dancing with the light from the tank. I didn't know what to say, so I said nothing. I felt his arm slip around my shoulders, and I smiled slightly. His arms were big and strong even in sickness. Silently, he pulled me a little closer, and I closed my eyes, not wanting to forget that moment.

I HAD NO CLEAR DIRECTION OR PLAN FOR MY LIFE, BUT WHAT I DIDN'T REALIZE WAS THAT GOD HAD USED MY FATHER TO PLANT A SEED IN ME. AND EVEN THOUGH IT WOULD LIE DORMANT FOR MANY YEARS, IT WAS THERE, WAITING FOR THE RIGHT TIME TO EMERGE.

I didn't know it at the time, but in that moment a seed had been planted.

When I was 13, my father died. The last thing we did together was get baptized. It took several men to help my father in and out of the water, his body, frail, small, and ravaged with cancer. After the ceremony they gave each of us a small Bible to mark the occasion. When I got home I placed the book into a box in my closet for safekeeping.

After my father passed, we moved to Atlanta. My mother had found work, and we all needed a fresh start. Maybe we were running a bit, trying to forget what happened. Trying to get away from familiar surroundings, from places that would remind us of him, of what had been taken from us.

I was angry with God for taking my father, and my faith soon faded into the past, long forgotten. I struggled to find purpose and meaning in a world that seemed full of doubt, uncertainty, cruelty, and pain. I had no clear direction or plan for my life, but what I didn't realize was that God had used my father to plant a seed in me. And even though it would lie dormant for many years, it was there, waiting for the right time to emerge.

That wouldn't happen for almost two decades.

It was my second year in college, and I had been ignoring God for too long. I went to my closet and opened a small, dusty box. Inside was the Bible I had received when my father and I had been baptized. I started to read. I don't know why, but I hoped that in those pages I would find some direction. **WHAT AM I GOING TO CHASE WITH THE DAYS GIVEN TO ME?**

Over the next few years, my faith and understanding of Scripture took on new clarity. Life took on a new perspective, and I started asking the question, what am I going to chase with the days given to me?

I prayed for purpose in my life. God began to orchestrate events in my life, and He started with making me a police officer.

"Hey you, stop right there!" I yelled out the window of my police cruiser. It was springtime in the South, and I was about to catch a thief in the middle of the night.

I flashed a light on the young man and caught his attention. He stared for a second and then pulled hard on the hanger he had slid between the parked car's window and doorframe. He jerked once, and his hand slipped off the hanger. He tried again, and this time the wire came free. He turned and ran into the darkness behind the car.

I slammed the cruiser into gear and jumped out. My boots felt heavy, and the weight of my belt, handcuffs, gun, baton, and radio made me feel awkward, slow, and clumsy. Still, I ran hard behind the house I thought he'd ducked behind.

I turned the corner between two houses and plunged into the darkness. An eight-foot fence blocked the narrow passage into the backyard and huddled in the corner was my target. Tommy was 15 years old. His eyes were wide and unblinking. He still held the wire coat hanger, both hands clasped together around the thin piece of metal as if in prayer.

"Where are your parents?" I asked him sternly. Silence. "Where are your parents?" I asked again, louder. I took a step toward him, my flashlight square in his face.

"I don't know," he replied meekly. "I live with my grandmother."

"Does she know where you are?"

"No, sir."

"Do you know her phone number?"

"We don't have a phone. Can't afford it."

I paused, and my tone softened. I'd met kids like him before. "OK," I said angling the light away from his face. "I'll drive you home." Home for Tommy was a government housing project on the south side of the city. It was the middle of the night, and I recognized several drug dealers walking the streets as we arrived.

"Is this your grandson?" I asked the tired, elderly woman who answered the door. We had awakened her. It was almost 2:00 a.m.

"Yes, it is," she said to me and then turning to the boy, calmly said, "Get inside and get to bed." She was not angry and didn't stop to even ask why I had brought her grandson home. She simply said, "Thank you," and closed the door.

I stood on their porch for a couple minutes marveling at what had just happened. And for the next few nights, I couldn't get Tommy out of my mind. Where were his parents? Why doesn't his grandmother care that a police officer brought him home in the middle of the night? What is going to happen to this kid? What is his future?

Something was stirring in me.

Finally, I could take it no more. A few days later I drove out to the housing project and knocked on the old aluminum screen door.

"Hey, Tommy, come here." I said as friendly as I could. I smiled as he looked up. He was visibly nervous, but he walked to my car. "I have a job for you. I need someone to mow my lawn. Would you like to make some money?"

Tommy stared at me for a moment. He looked skeptical, but then something in him told him it would be OK. I could see the wheels spinning in his mind. A little extra cash would be nice. He nodded.

"OK, I'll pick you up tomorrow morning."

I didn't have much extra money (my annual income was less than $17,000), but I hired him anyway. I had to do something. And every week for the next several months, Tommy would come, and we would work on my lawn together. We talked about life, his home situation, school, and slowly we became friends. **GOD'S SEED WAS STARTING TO GROW.** I shared with him that God loved him and wanted a relationship with him. And every time we got together, I remembered the many moments I had with my father.

Tommy and I were from two different worlds, but I spoke into his life the best I could. Every week I looked forward to those times working together. I didn't know it then, but God's seed was starting to grow.

How did a cop from Atlanta end up working with young men in West Virginia?

I think there were several factors—tools, if you will—God provided over the years, but the first and perhaps most important thing He did was to plant a seed in my heart. Some people might refer to it as a dream or ambition. I think a seed is very different from a personal ambition or goal. A seed comes from outside a person.

A SEED IS VERY DIFFERENT FROM A PERSONAL AMBITION OR GOAL. A SEED COMES FROM OUTSIDE A PERSON. IT IS PLANTED BY SOMEONE ELSE. IT IS NURTURED BY A GARDENER OVER TIME.

It is planted by someone else. It is nurtured by a gardener over time. And we don't always know or understand how it grows.

In my case, I believe the vision for a boys' home was something God, through my father, planted in me. I don't think it was my idea or even my original desire. I think it was all from God.

It may seem like a minor distinction, but I think there are at least four key defining characteristics of a seed that distinguish it from a simple ambition or passion. And if a leader wants to follow God, they must evaluate whether or not what they are doing is growing from a God-planted seed or their own desires.

First of all, I think any seed or vision planted by God is going to be related to the gospel and the building of the kingdom of God. In Matthew 28, as Jesus was getting ready to leave this earth, He gave His disciples some pretty clear marching orders:

> Then Jesus came to them and said, "All authority in heaven and on earth has been given to me. Therefore go and make disciples of all nations, baptizing them in the name of the Father and of the Son and of the Holy Spirit, and teaching them to obey everything I have commanded you."
> —Matthew 28:18–20

It makes no sense that a vision given by God would not be related in some way to the fulfillment of and obedience to this command. I don't think it is wrong to have other dreams and personal ambitions, but I don't think they are the same thing as a seed from God.

Recently, a young couple asked to meet with my wife (Dawn) and me about a vision they had for a sustainable farm. As we sat in my office, I asked them to tell me what they had in mind.

"Well," the young man started to tell us, "we just really want to make a place that really considers how we are using the planet, being good stewards of what God has given us."

"That's great," I replied, "but I am not sure this is what God is calling you to do."

"Why not?" his wife asked, a bit concerned.

"Well, where's the gospel?" I asked. "God wants people to know Him through Jesus, and while your intentions are pure and even good, I don't think God would call you to something or put something in your heart that doesn't accomplish that goal."

It was pretty clear they hadn't considered that point, and I am happy to say they left that meeting with the words, "You're right. We're going to go figure that out. We want this to be from God, not us."

A seed is, foremost, something that God plants, and His intention is to grow His kingdom, for people to know the gospel, to know Jesus died so we could be forgiven and called the children of God. I believe any vision without the gospel is simply not a vision from God.

Second, I think a seed is something only God can nurture. When I look back over my life, I can see certain events that I believe God orchestrated: my father sharing with me his vision of a boys' home in West Virginia not long before his death, my time on the police force, and witnessing the plight of so many young men like Tommy.

And there were other stories along the way.

Once I got called to a Waffle House to break up a gang of kids that were reportedly in the middle of a big fight. When I got there, I encountered something I never anticipated. It wasn't a gang, it was a youth group, and they were playing Nerf football in the parking lot.

I found the leader and told him we had received some complaints He was embarrassed and apologetic, telling me he was sorry, and they would calm down right away. I asked him the name of their group.

"Young Life," he told me and then added quickly, "Please don't report us to the national office."

I laughed and told him I was a Christian too. As the kids started cleaning up from horsing around, he told me how he volunteered with Young Life because they went to where the kids were and shared the love of Christ with them. And they had a lot of fun in the process.

I think he could tell I was impressed because as he turned to leave he reached into his pocket and gave me his card. "You know what?" he said, "You'd make a great youth group leader, with your background as a cop and being a Christian. You should come down and see what we're doing with these inner-city kids."

I took his card and put it in my pocket. At that moment, I felt a tug on my heart and wondered at how strange the night had become. I had been prepared to break up a fight and instead left wondering if God was leading me in a new direction. I never could have planned or orchestrated that meeting.

Two weeks passed, then three. I held on to that card for more than a month, but I never called. I was too afraid. God still had some nurturing to do to the seed He planted. Only God could have done that, and yet it was instrumental in moving me toward West Virginia and Chestnut Mountain Ranch.

Third, when God plants a seed, only He understands the time it will take to be fruitful. And usually that is not overnight.

In South America there is a plant called the Queen of the Andes. It is an amazing plant because it grows very slowly. For most of its life, anywhere from 80 to 150 years, the plant basically sits dormant. It shows no growth, does not flower, and produces no fruit. It simply waits.

And then suddenly, at just the right time, at just the time God intends, it explodes, growing to more than 30 feet tall, a towering stem that may contain in excess of 8,000 blooms. It takes a while, but when it finally happens it is spectacular event.

I can't say with certainty, but my sense is that any seed planted by God in your heart is going to be nurtured and fostered over a period of time before it blossoms and brings forth fruit. It will be the product of events and conversations that have spanned the course of your life. When I think back on the events that led me to found Chestnut Mountain Ranch, I can see how God planted the seed and, step-by-step, developed the vision in me.

When we recognize that a seed is something God nurtures over time, perhaps a long time, it enables us to be patient with the process. Sometimes, when we have a personal ambition or vision, we rush to see it achieved. Maybe we are afraid our zeal will wane or an opportunity will pass and be gone forever, so we rush to get things rolling.

I have found that when a vision is from God, the immediacy and urgency of the situation dissipates. God knows the right timing. He knows when things need to bloom and the fruit need to appear. For each of us there is a time to wait and a time to act, but the timeline is different for each person. Until then, we can let the seed remain in the ground.

After a couple of years on the police force, I was promoted to a street crimes unit. Our unit's job took us into some of the roughest neighborhoods of metro Atlanta. I saw firsthand the devastating effects of fatherless homes, and how young men with no dreams or hope for a future might end up in gangs and embracing destructive life patterns.

It broke my heart, so I scheduled a meeting with a pastor at my church, 12Stone, to talk more about this growing vision of a boys' home. As I sat down with Chris Huff and explained what I had in mind, he was excited for me and encouraging, but his advice was not what I expected.

"I think you need to wait," he said. "I don't think God has you quite ready yet."

It was not what I wanted to hear, but I knew that if this desire to help young men was truly from God, then I could trust that His timing would be perfect. I would wait for Him to cause that seed to flower. I didn't know how long it would take or what the next step would be, but I had a peace knowing it was in God's hands.

In the following years, Dawn and I would talk about what God had planned for us. What if we worked in Africa? What if we became missionaries to Jamaica? What if we worked with troubled youth? We were open to wherever God would lead, even taking a stint in the children's nursery at church—a tough place for a man who weighs in at 240 pounds and is six foot five. We were waiting, and while we were waiting, we tested a few options, looking for the right open door.

Finally, you know it is a seed from God when it becomes something you cannot ignore. Two more events finally convinced me that we needed to move toward working full-time with troubled boys. God was calling us in that direction.

My work with the police street crimes unit continued to bring me face-to-face with many young men headed in the wrong direction. With little to no guidance, many of these kids' lives were ending too early, either through death or incarceration. I was doing all I could as an officer, but my heart longed to do more, to offer some sort of help. But I didn't know what to do or how I could help. All I knew was how to enforce the law. And I only had one lawn that needed mowing. I met dozens of kids who needed help.

During some of my patrols, I was taken into an especially rough part of the city. There were lots of abandoned houses, and one day I noticed a man on a motorcycle pulling up to a house I knew had been empty for a couple years. This seemed out of place, so I drove up and called out to him to ask what he was doing.

"Oh, I live here," he said, smiling. "My name is Richard. I just graduated from Appalachian Bible College in West Virginia, and I am working with some kids in another part of the city."

Call it coincidence if you want, but over the next several months Richard and I would meet and talk on the porch of that old dilapidated house. I told him about all the boys I was encountering on the street and how I felt like they needed someone in their lives.

"I think it's you, Steve," he told me one afternoon. "I think God is calling you to reach out to boys like that."

I laughed dismissively and went home. But I couldn't shake the thought from my mind. A couple weeks later, I went back hoping to catch him. No one was there. I peered in the window of the old house. It looked like it had been deserted for years. No trace of anyone. I never saw Richard again.

Not long after that, on Mother's Day at a local restaurant, I ran into a fellow officer, Joe LaRocco, who I had not seen in a few years. I asked him where he was stationed, and he shook his head. "I'm not a cop anymore," he said. "My wife and I became houseparents at a children's home called Eagle Ranch." I looked at him stunned, unable to answer. "You all should come for a visit." We exchanged phone numbers, and some excitement began to stir as Dawn and I prepared to visit a children's home. We had been praying about what God would have us do in our lives. Now, after a solid year of praying, we began to see some doors opening. I absolutely loved my career in law enforcement, and I would have been happy wearing the badge for a lifetime, but when God stirs in unique ways the "calling" becomes an adventure.

As scared as I was about going into ministry, about finances, about and how this would affect our marriage and family, as unprepared as I felt, I could no longer doubt the direction God was moving.

He had nurtured the seed for many years—from those late-night talks with my dad to all the kids I saw to Tommy mowing my yard to the Young Life leader at Waffle House to Richard the Bible college graduate. I knew that I couldn't ignore what had happened and what God was calling us to.

The next week we went to see Joe and his family at Eagle Ranch. One month later, I turned in my badge, and we moved into a home as new houseparents with seven new sons.

The Bible offers many examples of men and women in whom God planted a seed, a vision for bringing about His kingdom and announcing the gospel to the world. In most cases, the seed took a long time to grow and bloom. It was just the first step in the process, but it was vital because it was borne both of God and about God.

Saved from infanticide by the bold actions of his mother, Moses grew up in Pharaoh's house, escaping the enslavement his fellow Hebrews endured in Egypt. The Book of Exodus tells us that one day, after he had grown up, Moses went out to where his own people were working. He saw an Egyptian severely beating a Hebrew slave.

In all honestly, it probably wasn't the first time he had witnessed such cruelty, but this time it struck a chord. He was moved deeply by the injustice. He couldn't simply stand by and do nothing. And so "looking this way and that and seeing no one, he killed the Egyptian and hid him in the sand" (Exodus 2:12).

I cannot say his actions were justified or that he went about things in the right way, but one thing is for sure: a seed had been planted in Moses. He had seen the suffering of his people, of God's people, and it moved him.

He was in no way ready at that time to step into the role God had for him; the seed needed time to germinate and grow. Moses would soon flee Egypt and go to Midian. He would tend sheep for 40 years before God would call him back to rescue His people.

Hundreds of years later, Nehemiah, an Israelite, was in exile in Persia with the rest of Israel, when one of his brothers came from Judah with news from home. The word was not good: "Those who survived the exile and are back in the province are in great trouble and disgrace. The wall of Jerusalem is broken down, and its gates have been burned with fire" (Nehemiah 1:3).

In those days, a city was only as strong as its walls and gates. They provided the means of defense and were the security for all who lived there. The reputation of a city was nearly synonymous with the strength of its walls. And Jerusalem was in bad shape.

This was especially significant for Nehemiah because Jerusalem was no ordinary city—it was the city of God. It was the place on earth that God chose to reside, the city upon which He had put His own name. For Jerusalem to be in disrepair was not only dangerous to those living there, it was a disgrace to God Himself. It made God look bad. And that was not something Nehemiah could just ignore. He was moved, and a seed had been planted.

He writes, "When I heard these things, I sat down and wept. For some days I mourned and fasted and prayed before the God of heaven" (v. 4).

There may not be a more dramatic seed-planting than what happened to Saul, who later became known as Paul. A zealous persecutor of the early church, Saul was on his way to Damascus on a mission to jail Christians when a heavenly light flashed, knocking him to the ground. Eventually, Saul would become a vital cog in God's plan for the spreading of the gospel to the Gentiles.

I don't know how much of this revelation Ananias told Saul when they met, but it is clear that Jesus planted a seed on that road and God used Ananias to strengthen that calling. Ananias healed Saul, and he was filled with the Holy Spirit. Saul was never the same after that.

Another example is Josiah, who became king of Israel when he was eight years old. Second Chronicles tells us he reigned for 31 years, and "he did what was right in the eyes of the LORD and followed the ways of his father David, not turning aside to the right or to the left" (2 Chronicles 34:2). We read on to learn that when he was just 16, he began to seek to God, and by the time he was 20, he started to purge Israel of all the idols and foreign gods prevalent in the land at the time.

Josiah did not come from a good family. His father, Amon, had been assassinated in his palace by his own officials who had conspired against him. He was an evil and prideful man who worshipped false gods and idols. He was not humble before God, which ultimately lead to his demise. Maybe this was the seed that God planted in Josiah.

Josiah's grandfather was Manasseh. He too was evil, following the pagan practices of foreign nations. He erected temples to the gods Baal and Asherah. He even went so far as to put a graven image in God's temple. Not a good idea. God raised up the Assyrians who took Manasseh prisoner, "put a hook in his nose, bound him with bronze shackles and took him to Babylon" (2 Chronicles 33:11).

Manasseh learned his lesson and "humbled himself greatly before the God of his ancestors" (v. 12). God listened to his plea and brought him back to his kingdom in Jerusalem where he rebuilt walls, removed foreign gods, and restored proper worship of God in the city. He died humbled, and the throne was passed to Amon.

It is entirely possible that a seed was planted in Josiah as he was undoubtedly told of the exile of his grandfather, his rebellion and the humility before God and how his kingdom was eventually restored. And surely he knew his father had failed, returning to worshipping foreign gods, and refusing to be humble. Josiah no doubt made the connection to his own father's murderous end.

I am drawn to the story of Josiah because his father and grandfather played no small part in planting the seed God had for his life.

My father planted a seed from God in me when I was about the same age as Josiah. And my vision is to carry that on in the lives of boys who come to us at Chestnut Mountain Ranch.

Josiah's seed—to follow and bring honor to God as king—grew over time. At 16 he sought God. At 20 he tore down carved idols and foreign altars, crushing them to dust and mixing it with the ground bones of the pagan priests who had overseen them. He wanted nothing left. At 26 he began to repair the Temple of the Lord. It was during those renovations that workers discovered a Book of the Law that would eventually lead to revival in all Israel. Josiah's seed was planted at a young age and grew slowly but eventually brought great honor to God and His kingdom. That's how it works.

> *Josiah removed all the detestable idols from all the territory belonging to the Israelites, and he had all who were present in Israel serve the LORD their God. As long as he lived, they did not fail to follow the LORD, the God of their ancestors.*
> —*2 Chronicles 34:33*

When we lived in Atlanta, Dawn and I attended 12Stone Church. While there, I had the privilege of being mentored by one of the pastors, Dan Reiland. Dan has spent his life studying the gift of leadership and has poured countless hours raising up new leaders.

One day, Dan gave me a blank piece of paper. Then he said, "Steve, I want you to write at the top of this page the following phrase: *My life's purpose is . . .*" I wrote out the words in black ink, looked at the page for a moment, then back at Dan, hoping he would help me fill in the rest. Instead he told me, "You have the next 12 months to write something down."

My discovery of the seed God had given me did not happen overnight. It took months of reflection and prayer to realize what God wanted me to do. God had been slowly directing me along a path that, for most of the time, had not been clear. I didn't realize what He had been doing, but as I looked back on the key moments of my life, things suddenly snapped into focus. And I knew beyond a shadow of a doubt what I needed to do.

From time to time, people will call me and ask for a meeting. They want to run an idea by me for a new venture or ministry. These are always exciting meetings for me because I love the enthusiasm and desire of people who want to make a difference in the world. And I want to encourage people to be all that God has called them to be.

My hope is that this is why you've picked up this book: to make a difference in the world for God, to share His message of salvation through Jesus, and to help spread the gospel and expand the kingdom. Every Christian should seek out their part in this mission. It is a command given to all of us. We just have to figure out what our place is in the bigger story.

If you're ready to jump in, to find the seed God has planted in you, ask yourself four questions. I think these questions (and lots of prayer and reflection and discussion and patience) will help you figure out where you need to concentrate your efforts. They will help you finish that sentence, *My life's purpose is . . .*

QUESTION 1:
WHAT ARE THE EVENTS OF YOUR LIFE THAT MOST SHAPED WHO YOU ARE TODAY?

I have shared many of the moments that most shaped my life. The late-night, early-morning talks with my father, my time as a police officer in Atlanta, and especially the unusual lawn-mowing partnership I had with Tommy. Then there were the encounters with the Young Life leader at the Waffle House, Richard the Bible college graduate, my chance meeting with Joe LaRocco, and our introduction to Eagle Ranch. And there were other key events and milestones that I will share throughout this book that were part of our journey.

Here's an exercise: Write down the most important and impactful events of your whole life—the times, conversations, and moments most vivid to you. They could be painful or joyous or sad or encouraging, but they should come to you pretty quickly.

Once you have them written down, see if you can find a common thread, something that ties them all together. In my case, I kept running into young men and young women who had lost or never had a strong adult presence in their life and were heading in the wrong direction. Or I met people who were doing whatever they could to help those kind of kids.

An oft-repeated command in the Bible is *to remember*. Throughout the Old and New Testament, God's people are encouraged and reminded to remember all God has done for them: how He liberated them from slavery in Egypt, how He brought them miraculously through the Red Sea, and how He brought them into a new and wonderful land that they could pass on to their children for generations.

Spend some time remembering what God has taken you through in your life. God planted His seed in you long ago, and you will only discover it if you take the time to look back and see the path He has taken you on.

QUESTION 2:

HOW HAVE THOSE EXPERIENCES MOVED YOUR HEART FOR THE GOSPEL AND THE KINGDOM OF GOD?

There are countless ambitious people in the world—entrepreneurs, businessmen and businesswomen, philanthropists—and they have made enormous impacts, both good and bad, on the world. But there is a difference between a seed that God plants and a desire or ambition of our own.

In order to fully realize our purpose and meaning in life, we have to be connected to God and specifically His mission and vision. This is what we were created for and why we were grafted into His family in the first place.

Paul, writing to the church in Ephesus, explains God's intention toward us pretty clearly:

> *But because of his great love for us, God, who is rich in mercy, made us alive with Christ even when we were dead in transgressions—it is by grace you have been saved. And God raised us up with Christ and seated us with him in the heavenly realms in Christ Jesus, in order that in the coming ages he might show the incomparable riches of his grace, expressed in his kindness to us in Christ Jesus. For it is by grace you have been saved, through faith—and this is not from yourselves, it is the gift of God—not by works, so that no one can boast. For we are God's handiwork, created in Christ Jesus to do good works, which God prepared in advance for us to do.*
>
> *—Ephesians 2:4-10*

Because of God's love for us, He saved us, seated us with Jesus, and now has some things for us to do. Things He prepared, a seed tied to His kingdom and His gospel and the good work He has done for all humanity through Jesus. Our good work, then, should be tied to God's good work.

As I grew up, my heart was torn for young people who needed guidance, but I also knew that I would be doing them a disservice if I didn't introduce them to Jesus, the ultimate Guide, the only one who could truly rescue them, lead them, and bring them the kind of joy, happiness, and meaning I so desperately wanted for each of them. Central to the mission of Chestnut Mountain Ranch is introducing each boy to Jesus and teaching him to be a lifelong follower and worker in the kingdom.

Maybe you want to bring water to the people of Africa or rescue animals from abusive homes (both of which are really good things), but if you are not more motivated that people know Jesus, then your idea may not be a seed from God.

QUESTION 3:
HOW HAS GOD USED HIS WORD AND PRAYER TO PREPARE YOU FOR THE WORK HE HAS CALLED YOU TO?

Early on in my faith journey I read 2 Timothy 2:15:

> *Do your best to present yourself to God as one approved, a worker who does not need to be ashamed and who correctly handles the word of truth.*

As an officer I saw firsthand the difficulty many kids were having and understood their world and the challenges they were facing. In my days on the force God started to teach me how to relate to young men and women from those circumstances. I began to understand how to be "a worker who does not need to be ashamed" when it mattered, and when to "correctly handle the word of truth."

When I was in college, because I felt so directionless, I developed a real thirst for God's Word and prayer. I didn't know where else to turn or what else to do, so I studied and prayed. Those years were foundational and provided much-needed discipline, perseverance, and knowledge for my current ministry.

If God has planted a seed in you, He will confirm and develop that seed as you study the Bible and pray.

QUESTION 4:
WHAT IS STOPPING YOU?

In Matthew 13, Jesus tells a parable about a farmer who goes out to sow seeds. It is a familiar story, and maybe you remember that the seeds fall on four kinds of soil: a path with no soil, a rocky path, among the thorns, and finally on good soil.

Only one quarter of the seeds that were sown actually grew and bloomed and produced any kind of fruit. The rest were wasted, ruined before they could mature and achieve their purpose. There are situations, things that get in the way.

The same could be true of the seed God has planted in you.

Jesus explains the meaning behind the story to His followers. The seed sown on the path finds no soil and is quickly stolen away by Satan. The seed in the soil among the rocks has no roots, no foundation or depth, and when trials come it fades and withers. The seed that finds itself among the thorns is choked out, distracted by wealth and the desire for other things. Only the good soil, the heart that accepts the seed, produces fruit.

This parable teaches us there are things that will stop God's seed from taking root in our lives. Satan distracts many from the calling we have to fight for the gospel and the kingdom of God. He steals the good works God has planted, the desire to help and make the world a better place, and takes them in another direction.

Many people are impatient. They do not take the time to prepare properly, to grow deep roots and trust that, in time, God will bring their vision to fruition. If you try to short-circuit the process, you may be eventually derailed by trouble and persecution that are sure to come.

Everyone wants financial security, but concern over money can keep and has kept the best seeds from growing. It can keep you from starting up your ministry or, equally debilitating, become its focus. I can't tell you how many leaders of various ministries and movements spend the vast majority of their time worried about and consumed by financial matters. It is enough to kill any seed from God.

Most of us will get stopped by one of those conditions. Only one out of four, if we take this passage to heart, will see their seed grow and be fruitful. My prayer is this will be you.

TOOL NO. 2:
REFINEMENT

speak at a lot of churches. It is an honor to get to share my story and the story of what God is doing in and through Chestnut Mountain Ranch. My hope is to encourage the churches I visit, and I hope that they see if God can use an ex-cop from Atlanta, then He can certainly use them in great ways for the kingdom. Many times after a service, a young man or woman will approach me, and I can usually anticipate the questions: I have a dream. How do I know it is from God, and how do I know when I am ready?

Put another way: How do I discern God's will for my life, and how do I know when I am ready? These are questions a lot of us have and ones that deserve careful consideration.

One of my favorite passages of Scripture is found in Romans 12. Here, Paul writes pretty clearly about the process of figuring out God's will for your life.

> *Therefore, I urge you, brothers and sisters, in view of God's mercy, to offer your bodies as a living sacrifice, holy and pleasing to God—this is your true and proper worship. Do not conform to the pattern of this world, but be transformed by the renewing of your mind. Then you will be able to test and approve what God's will is—his good, pleasing and perfect will.*
>
> —Romans 12:1–2

Paul suggests practical, if not difficult, things we can do to "test and approve" God's will in our lives. We have to lay down our lives, we have to not conform to the world, and we have to think differently about the world: we have to "renew our minds."

Simple, right?

Not really. It is actually difficult and takes nearly our whole lives to complete. In fact, we will probably be laying our lives down, not conforming, and renewing our thinking until we meet Jesus in heaven.

I see this process as refinement. It is a gradual stripping, grinding down, readjusting, and fine-tuning how we see ourselves, God, and the sin-filled world we live in that eventually leads us into God's will for our lives.

As I looked back on my own journey, I realized I needed God to make some adjustments in my life and the way I looked at things before He could send us out to start Chestnut Mountain Ranch. I needed to better understand what it meant to offer myself as a living sacrifice, to not conform any longer to the pattern of this world, and to renew my mind, my way of thinking about God.

It's taken some time, and I have by no means arrived. But I can see clear evidence of the process of refinement God has taken me through.

"You want us to do what?" I looked at Dawn and could hardly believe the words that had come out of her mouth. *Say that again,* I thought, *I dare you.* We only had been married a few years. It was the year 2000, and our daughter was not even a year old—I was a newbie to the idea of taking care of babies.

"I think we should volunteer for the nursery at church."

I shook my head, pounding one side then the other to loosen any foreign object that might have been blocking my hearing. "Are you serious?" I asked, completely shocked and in disbelief. "Look at me! It is very likely that I will step on some kid and crush him like a bug. I won't even know until I get home and take off my shoes and have to scrape him off with a spatula."

Dawn rolled her eyes, but it didn't deter me one bit.

"What self-respecting mother would leave their beloved child with the Jolly Green Giant here? There's no way we would get approved by the accreditation board. I think Child Protective Services would get involved." Now I was just being ridiculous.

"We're doing this," Dawn reiterated. "There is a real need for people to help, and we're available."

I don't remember if this is exactly how the conversation went (probably not!), but I do remember feeling like I was way out of my element taking care of those little kids. Do you remember the movie *Kindergarten Cop*, in which an enormous Arnold Schwarzenegger goes undercover as a teacher? It is a total disaster; he has no idea what he is doing and is humiliated in about every possible way by those kids.

That is about how I felt. Clueless, humbled, humiliated. But this was the door God opened for us. And so we put aside our desires, and we walked through and served. I believe God wanted us to lay our lives down on that altar in a very tangible and practical way. He needed to see us do it, and we needed to experience what that was like. It was an important part of the refinement process for us and for me in particular.

GOD CAN USE YOUR SKILLS AND ABILITIES, WITHOUT A DOUBT. BUT WHAT GOD WANTS FIRST, EVEN BEFORE YOUR TALENT, IS YOUR HEART.

When Paul encourages the church at Rome to offer their bodies as living sacrifices in Romans 12, he was asking them to adjust and refine how they view themselves. Often, when we have a vision or are feeling a call from God, we assume it is because we are talented or gifted or have something special to bring to the table. God calls us, we think, because He needs us.

God can use your skills and abilities, without a doubt. But what God wants first, even before your talent, is your heart. Are you willing to do whatever He wants you to do? Are you willing to lay your life down on the altar? Or do you only want to do what you want to do?

To figure this out, God takes us through a process of opening doors that may seem wrong for us at the time. I wasn't ultimately called to be a long-term nursery worker, but at that time, God opened that door because, I believe, He wanted to see if I would go through it. Would I be obedient, lay down my life, and be humble enough to do His will? Would I offer my life as a living sacrifice?

I didn't know it, but working for two years in that nursery was a crucial part of my refinement process. I was learning to lay down my life, a skill I was really going to need down the road.

When my father was diagnosed with cancer, I noticed a real change in him. Suddenly, things that had once been important to him no longer seemed to matter as much. He had always been a man driven to succeed, to excel in his career. But when the cancer hit, I think his thought process changed. He started to read his Bible more, really searching the Scriptures to know God. He also started to care about people a lot more. It was then that he started coming in to my room late at night to talk, to see how I was doing, to really get to know me and what was going on in my world. I saw a man who was being refined, who was realizing that, in the days he had left, he was going to lay aside himself and invest in what mattered most: God and the people around him.

Paul's writing in Romans and my father's transformation remind me of Moses's prayer recorded in Psalm 90: "Teach us to number our days, that we may gain a heart of wisdom" (v. 12).

Moses understood that our lives are brief. They soon come to an end, and if we will have a correct perspective on who we are, that goes a long way in us gaining wisdom, which is God's perspective. I think the person who understands the brevity of life is most willing to lay it on the altar before God. And when we lay down our lives—

Moses struggled with this a bit himself, not wanting to follow God's leading—God reveals, in that act, His will for us.

I am not sure how it exactly works, but I do know that God worked on me and got me to the place where I said, "I will serve wherever you want me to, even in a nursery." He started to open doors and reveal even clearer the direction He had for me.

Dawn probably had this figured out from the beginning, which is why she signed us up, but she's a lot smarter and more refined than me.

A couple of years after I came onto the police force, we were given new patrol cars: Pontiac Grand Am GTs. They were really sharp-looking automobiles and very fast. Everyone was pretty excited about the potential and how helpful these new machines would be in the field.

I remember the first week my partner and I had the new cars out on patrol, we got a call from dispatch about a burglary in progress. We were close to the scene, so we made a quick U-turn and headed that direction. As we arrived, we saw a black car leaving in a big hurry.

That was probably our guy; we called in and began pursuit.

This was the first time we really got to test out the capabilities of our new cruisers, and I'd be lying if I said we weren't both anxious to see what these things could do in the line of duty under real-life circumstances.

After a couple quick turns, our suspect got on to a major interstate that led into the heart of the city. It was well after midnight, so fortunately traffic was light. Once on the highway, things sped up considerably, and almost immediately we could see the car start to accelerate and pull away.

But we had the upper hand, or so we thought. I pressed on the accelerator, and we could feel the engine growl and dig in, throwing us back in our seats. We shot quickly into the night—50, 60, then 70 miles per hour. We steadily sped up, gaining on the suspect—90 miles per hour—he was getting closer, coming back to us, but still a half mile in front. Steadily we climbed over 100 miles per hour, and I still kept the pedal down, pushing it to the floor.

The street lamps were just a blur, and the well-engineered car pulled tight and low to the road. We were getting close. I pushed a little harder, then click; it was as if someone had shut off the lights. We lost power, the car started to coast, we lost speed, and the black car sped off in front of us.

I kept my foot to the floor, checking the gauges and dials to see if there was an emergency alert. Everything seemed to be in working order. Still we drifted: 90 down to 80. My partner and I looked at each other, neither of us knowing what was happening.

At 75 we felt like we were crawling at a snail's pace: then we hit 70 miles per hour and heard another click. The car reengaged, and we starting to gain speed again. We shrugged at each other, and I pressed on the pedal hoping to catch up for the lost time.

But as soon as we hit 105, the car shut down again. We drifted back to 70 miles per hour when it would reengage. We didn't realize it at the time, but I remember learning later that the manufacturer had installed governors that would shut down the engine when it reached certain speeds. These were designed to protect both the engine and the drivers. The only problem was that it kept us, the police, from doing our jobs.

And we knew we couldn't be successful, to do what we had been called to do, until those restrictors were removed.

PART OF THE REFINEMENT PROCESS FOR US IS THE REMOVAL OF THINGS THAT HINDER US FROM KNOWING, AND FOLLOWING, GOD'S WILL FOR OUR LIVES.

Part of the refinement process for us is the removal of things that hinder us from knowing, and following, God's will for our lives. Paul writes, "Do not conform to the pattern of this world" (Romans 12:2).

The word *conform* comes from a root word that means to be associated with or a companion of this world. It means we have to throw off a certain way of thinking, a certain way of acting, if we are to know God's will. I think this means there are forces in the world that would distract, hold us back, and restrict our ability to accomplish what God would have for us.

In Hebrews, the writer—many people think it was the Apostle Paul speaking here—encourages his readers to "throw off everything that hinders and the sin that so easily entangles. And let us run with perseverance the race marked out for us" (Hebrews 12:1).

It is interesting that the writer mentions two things we need to throw off: "everything that hinders us" and "sin." I don't think they mean the same thing. My experience tells me there are two different but equally powerful forces we need to throw off during this refinement process: the first is our own sin and the second is the opposition of others that would entangle us and keep us from doing what God has told us to do.

Sin is pretty obvious. We all have a pretty good idea what areas we still hang onto—our pride and rebellion and disobedience. I know my weaknesses and the areas where God is dealing with me. In some places, I am more willing to be refined than in others. God is changing me, rooting out my sin, pointing out areas in which I need to grow so that I won't be hindered in the mission He has given me. I love the encouragement from Hebrews:

Moreover, we have all had human fathers who disciplined us and we respected them for it. How much more should we submit to the Father of our spirits and live! They disciplined us for a little while as they thought best; but God disciplines us for our good, in order that we may share in his holiness.

—*vv. 9–10*

That word *holiness* means to be "set apart," unencumbered by the things of this world, nonconformity in the best sense of the world. Regulators off so we can run at 100 miles per hour and faster.

So the throwing off of sin is a vital part of the refinement we need to know and accomplish God's will for us. The next part of that process is to remove from ourselves anything else that might hinder us.

When I first moved back to West Virginia in 2005, I was meeting with a lot of people, Christians and non-Christians, trying to rally support for what we were hoping to do. A friend introduced me to a pastor, who, I was told, had close to 3,000 acres of land. My friend thought he might be open to selling 200 or so for the ranch.

I was excited going in to the meeting because I was meeting with a brother in Christ, and I assumed that would put us on the same wavelength. We had the same Spirit directing us, so how could we not find a way to work together?

And I could not have been more wrong.

Maybe it was naive of me to think that all Christians are going to want to support and encourage one another. The Bible tells us we should, but that doesn't always make it so.

As I sat down with this gentleman and explained what we were trying to do, why we needed some land, and our hope that he might see a way to sell us some of his property, it soon became very evident we were not on anything even resembling the same wavelength.

His face became twisted and sour as he listened to me explain how West Virginia needed another boys' home and how, as a Christian, I felt called to reach out to families that were struggling and needed Jesus.

"You know what I think?" he asked, his face getting a little red around the edges. "I think you need to go back to Atlanta, where you came from. We can take care of our own here."

I was taken aback by his reaction, and I am sure he noticed the stunned look on my face. I tried to explain that I was from West Virginia and that in fact my family had settled in these hills back in the 1700s. This *was* my home. And, as gently as I could, I pointed out that we had not done a very good job of taking care of our kids. We'd done a pretty poor job, actually.

The conversation didn't last long after that. He reiterated that he didn't think West Virginia needed another boys' home, and there was nothing he could—or would—do to support a new one.

And good day to you, sir.

Now, there are times when you need to listen to good counsel; God will bring people into your life to direct you in certain ways. They will help you make decisions and find the proper course.

This was not one of those situations.

This was one of those times when I had to keep someone else's negativity and criticism from entangling and distracting me from the mission at hand. It would have been very easy to have gotten discouraged and let that meeting impact the founding of the ranch. If I had taken his criticisms to heart, I may have pulled up the tent stakes and gone home.

God used that man to help refine me, to help me see there were going to be detractors who would question my calling and what we were trying to accomplish. And that experience helped to toughen me up. Instead of debilitating me or causing me to doubt what I was doing, it strengthened my resolve and the conviction that I was on the right track.

And I think God will bring that kind of opposition from time to time, the kind that could entangle and trip you up, in order to refine you and deeply embed His calling on your life in your heart.

The story of Nehemiah is pretty incredible when you think about it. Here is a servant, exiled in a foreign land, a long, long way from home. He gets word that his hometown is not doing so well. The walls have fallen down; Jerusalem is in ruins and, quite frankly, a disgrace. The people who have survived the exile are in great trouble, and there seems to be no help on the way. It is a dire situation.

But what can Nehemiah do? He has no money, no influence; he is not even there. How can he possibly do anything about this situation? It surely seems like a lost cause.

But sometimes, when all seems hopeless, that is when things can really get going. I think Nehemiah does about the only thing he could in that circumstance. He prays.

> *When I heard these things [about the wall being destroyed and his countrymen in distress], I sat down and wept. For some days I mourned and fasted and prayed before the God of heaven.*
>
> *—Nehemiah 1:4*

I won't quote the entire prayer, but I think there are a few things to point out about it. First, Nehemiah recognized the greatness of God. He pointed out that God keeps His covenants of love with those who love Him and obey Him.

Second, Nehemiah confessed that he and all of Israel were sinful and their rebellion and wickedness was the reason they were in their current situation. Nehemiah takes all the blame for the downfall of Jerusalem—no shifting this blame on to God.

Third, Nehemiah reminded God of His promise to forgive the people if they would return to Him with their hearts; God would gather them from the farthest horizon. "I will gather them from there and bring them to the place I have chosen as a dwelling for my Name" (v. 9).

Finally, as a servant of God, redeemed by His strong hand, Nehemiah asks for God's help, fully recognizing that He can do something about the current crisis. In Nehemiah's case this meant favor from King Artaxerxes to go to Jerusalem with the needed materials.

We of course know the rest of the story: the king helped Nehemiah, and he was able to get the wall rebuilt. But put yourself in Nehemiah's shoes in that first chapter. It looked pretty bad. He had no plan, no resources, nothing.

I wonder how many possible ideas would have gone through my mind if I were faced with the same dilemma. I would have been scrolling through my phone contacts seeing if I had a buddy in construction or a lawyer who could sue the Babylonians for wrongful detainment. I think I would have been devising plan after plan, trying to think of a way I could get back to Jerusalem to make things right.

When Paul wrote to the Romans and told them they should be transformed by the renewing of their minds, I think this may be what he was talking about. If we want to know and understand God's will for us, we have to think differently about God. Our faith in Him must be increased, and even in the face of unthinkable odds, He should be our first option.

It is an important part of the refinement process to renew our minds so that when we are faced with difficult and dire situations, our first thought is to turn in faith to God, and not somewhere else. This isn't often our natural inclination. We try to figure things out without God. We do pretty well on our own, or so we think. But in order for us to know God's will, for it to be revealed to us, we need to renew our way of thinking. Our faith and trust in Him, for all things, must increase.

OUR FAITH AND TRUST IN HIM, FOR ALL THINGS, MUST INCREASE.

When I was a young cop on the force, I was pretty capable, or at least that is what I thought. I was quick on my feet, observant, and didn't get outsmarted very often. I am also a large man, so there were not too many people who could take me in a fight. That's part of the problem of being in your twenties—you get to thinking sometimes a little too highly of yourself.

It didn't help that after only six years on the force, I made detective. I won't say I was cocky, but I did have a pretty healthy self-esteem. And while that's not always bad, I think I had some growing to do, some refinement, if you will.

About two weeks after I was promoted, I was out attending to some work-related business and heading back to the station when a call came over the radio. It immediately caught my attention: attempted rape. Dispatch relayed that the situation had occurred not far from where I was. I immediately took a sharp left turn, and within five minutes I was on the scene, the first to arrive at a large office complex next to the Chattahoochee River. When I got out of my car, I saw a group of business people huddled around a young woman who appeared to be about 15 years old. Someone had given her a too-large T-shirt. Apparently her clothes had been ripped and were ruined, piled on the ground next to her.

When I met the group, I identified myself and thanked everyone for their help. Then I turned to the girl and asked her what happened. Her story astounded me.

"I was with my sister and cousins down by the river," she said with a thick South African accent. She was visiting family and had only been in the United States a short time.

"We were fishing," she continued. "It was such a nice day. We didn't think anyone would mind."

I jotted down a few notes. "What happened then?"

"We had been fishing for maybe 20 minutes when we heard someone call from the top of the embankment. It was a man's voice. He said that he needed to see our fishing licenses. We couldn't see anyone because of the brush, but he sounded very official."

I nodded as she continued.

"We didn't have a license. We didn't know you needed one. We were pretty scared we were going to get in trouble, but we thought it best we go meet this man and be honest that we didn't have a license."

"So you went up the bank?"

She nodded. "Yes, we started up. First my cousins, then my sister. I followed behind a bit."

She got quiet. I could see tears starting to form in the corners of her eyes. She looked down at the ground trying to regain her composure. I stood quietly, giving her a moment to regroup.

"He was naked," she said finally.

"What do you mean?" I asked, a little surprised.

"When we got to the top, we could see he didn't have on any clothes."

"So what did you do then?"

"We ran. My brother and sister were ahead of me, and they got away. But he grabbed me; he caught hold of my shirt and pulled me down. I screamed, but he held his hand over my mouth."

I nodded and said nothing. I wrote down what she told me. She stood still for a long time, staring blankly into space as if trying to not remember.

"Then what happened?" I finally broke the silence.

"He wrestled me to ground and got on top of me." She went silent again.

I didn't want to be insensitive to all this girl had gone through, but I had to ask, "Did he rape you?"

She shook her head no.

I was relieved but surprised. She was a tiny girl. I didn't see anyway she could have fended off any man with the obvious intent this one had.

"How did you get him off you?"

She paused and then looked up at me, her eyes staring directly into mine. "I said, 'In the name of Jesus, get off me.'"

This I did not expect.

"And it was as if a strong arm from heaven lifted and pushed that man right off me. And before I knew it, he was gone."

Over the course of the next several months, this young woman's story caught fire around Atlanta, and because I was the investigating detective, I was interviewed dozens of times by local media. And every time I was interviewed, almost without fail, I was asked how she was able to fight off her attacker. And I would tell them, "She said, 'In the name of Jesus, get off me.'"

Later, I learned her father was a pastor, and when we met he told me that from a very young age, they had taught their children to always have faith in God, to believe His name was powerful, and that faith in Him was all they needed.

All I could think was, *I do not have the kind of faith that that young girl has.*

God has done some refining in my life, and that has increased my faith. I have begun to rely less and less on my own talents and abilities, things we normally consider great assets, and to trust Him more and more like this girl from South Africa. Her story started a process of transformation in my mind, the way I think about God, the faith I have in Him.

Eddie Staub, founder of Eagle Ranch, is well known for saying, "Attempt something so great for God that it is doomed to failure unless God be in it," a quote that inspired him when he was taking his first steps of faith. It takes a different kind of mindset, one that has been refined and transformed, one that is full of faith and hope in God to be able to take on that kind of challenge.

It scares me to death to be honest, but I am thankful for people like Nehemiah, the girl from South Africa and her faith-filled parents, and for friends like Eddie who have shown me what the life of faith in God can be.

$25.54

I rubbed my eyes and then looked back at the piece of paper in my hand. It still said $25.54. I felt a slight squeeze in my chest, and my heart started to beat a little faster. I had just withdrawn $20 from the ATM, and the balance at the bottom of the receipt is what had caught my attention. I knew Dawn and I were running low in our accounts, but that was still a punch to the gut. That's all we had left. $25.54.

We were in our first year living in West Virginia. I had been working hard to make contacts and find support for Chestnut Mountain Ranch. We were living in a tiny run-down house out in the country, and our savings and the gifts we had received from friends and family were finally starting to run out. Well, they weren't running out; they had run out.

I'd be lying if I said this wasn't a stressful time, but looking back I realize that God uses difficult seasons to mold and shape our character, to refine us. I shouldn't be surprised by that; it is all over Scripture.

God wants to refine us, especially in the area of money. Obviously, He wants to refine us in many ways, but how we view, understand, and deal with money is right up there at the top. God warns us that we are probably going to have money issues in our lives, we are going to want to serve it, to trust it, to put our hope in it. We may get to the point where we think money could actually replace God, if we just had enough of it.

In fact, I have had people tell me that their lack of money for a ministry has been an indication that God was not in it. I don't think that's always true. Sometimes it is, but sometimes it may mean God is growing us in our view and reliance on money rather than Him. Over the years, God has kept me in what I call the "sweet spot," having enough money but not too much to where I don't have to trust in Him.

Jesus put it this way:

> *No one can serve two masters. Either you will hate the one and love the other, or you will be devoted to the one and despise the other. You cannot serve both God and money.*
>
> *—Matthew 6:24*

And that's why I think God will probably put you through the refinement process, especially when it comes to finances, or the lack thereof.

One of the most amazing stories in the Bible, in my opinion, happens when Jesus is with His disciples in the temple. They are standing opposite the treasury, the large box where people could put in their donations. They watch, from a distance, as many wealthy people came in and put in large amounts of money.

Ordinarily, this would be totally insignificant, but one woman with a small deposit catches Jesus' attention. From a worldly perspective, she put in far less—so much so that most people would not even notice. It was just a few cents. But not Jesus. In fact, He said this about her gift:

> Truly I tell you, this poor widow has put more into the treasury than all the others. They all gave out of their wealth; but she, out of her poverty, put in everything—all she had to live on.
>
> —Mark 12:43–44

Here's what is remarkable: she gave out of her poverty, all she had to live on. It boggles my mind that someone would do that. I don't remember what I did with that $25.54, but I'm pretty sure I didn't run out and donate it somewhere. For someone to give their last cent, all they had, shows a remarkable amount of faith. It shows someone who had complete and utter confidence in God to provide for their every need. It shows someone who has "renewed [their] mind" and thinks completely differently about money and God. I dare say, she had a pretty good idea about God and His will for her.

Is it fair to say this widow did not serve money but rather served God? I am not sure I could come up with a better example. Well, maybe Jesus, but you know . . .

I don't know if I recognized it then, but I believe now that low bank balance was God taking the time to refine me and my view of money. He wanted to see if I would trust Him when we had next to nothing. Was I serving Him or money? Where was my trust?

It is a good question to consider before launching a ministry or pursuing the call God has placed on your life. What is your view on money? Is it a point of stress in your life? Is a full bank account or total trust in God more important to you? You better answer honestly because chances are He will to test you in this.

I know people who seem to constantly talk about or complain about something related to money: the car has to get fixed and the kids need braces and the dog got worms again and those vets aren't cheap. It is nonstop and pretty obvious they haven't quite figured out they're headed down a path where their world—every decision and choice they make—is driven and controlled by money. And to me that sounds an awful lot like money has become their god.

God may have some work to do in your life—some refining—if money dominates your thoughts and is a constant worry. Only you can know for sure the degree to which that statement is a reflection of your life and thoughts, but if it is true or you are concerned that it may be, then I encourage you to spend some time talking with God about that. Maybe you will get lucky and He will take everything away from you and your only option will be to trust in Him.

It is pretty hard to have a lot of faith in something you don't have. You can lust after it, I suppose, but the faith part tends to wane.

How is a $25.54 bank account balance going to affect you?

Here's what it did for me: I prayed for three days straight. I didn't stop everything or even tell Dawn. I just prayed and trusted that God would provide what we needed. I had no idea where the money might come from, but I knew God brought us to West Virginia. And I didn't have any reason to believe that He was going to let us starve. I tried to remind myself of Jesus' Sermon on the Mount:

> So do not worry, saying, "What shall we eat?" or "What shall we drink?" or "What shall we wear?" For the pagans run after all these things, and your heavenly Father knows that you need them. But seek first his kingdom and his righteousness, and all these things will be given to you as well. Therefore do not worry about tomorrow, for tomorrow will worry about itself. Each day has enough trouble of its own.
>
> —Matthew 6:31–34

Food. Clothes. These are things that pagans, people who are not in the family of God, worry about. God's children shouldn't worry about such trivial matters. We should have a different mindset, a different way of thinking about things. And we should know that God will remember us.

It didn't come naturally. God had to teach me about that way of thinking, but over time and through this and many other experiences, I came to realize He would supply all our needs. We could serve Him and not worry about money. Somehow, almost out of money, I had peace. I knew He would provide.

After three days, I went to the end of our driveway to get the mail. Inside was a single envelope. It had no stamp, no address, just *Steve* handwritten in big, block letters on the front. I turned it over and saw inscribed, in the same block handwriting:

> *Let us not become weary in doing good, for at the proper time we will reap a harvest if we do not give up. Therefore, as we have opportunity, let us do good to all people, especially to those who belong to the family of believers.*
> —*Galatians 6:9–10*

Inside were ten crisp $50 bills.

At the end of that drive, next to that mailbox, I dropped to my knees and prayed, thanking God for remembering me. And for refining me, reminding me that I was His and He is mine, and that's all that I'll ever need.

TOOL NO. 3:
A TEAM

Dawn and I felt a unique calling to start a home modeled after Eagle Ranch. We had stepped out in faith when we left our careers and became houseparents at Eagle Ranch. We witnessed a program that truly worked. A ministry that was healing young men and restoring families. I always had a heart for West Virginia. After all, I was born there, and my family roots were deep in the mountain state, but I was determined to go where God led us. So, while we were still houseparents at Eagle Ranch, I began researching where the highest needs in the country were, and who had gone before us. After all, perhaps there was already an existing ministry to get plugged into.

West Virginia kept coming up in my research . . . poverty levels, family issues, drop-out rates, etc. I thought to myself, *This must be it!* Then I broke the news to my Southern-born-and-bred bride.

"Not West Virginia."

Dawn had a dead-set look in her eye that let me know she wasn't messing around.

"I thought when we took our vows, you said you would follow me anywhere," I countered with a playful grin creeping over the corners of my mouth. "I distinctly remember you saying that in front of God and everybody."

"Yeah, I meant anywhere except West Virginia." She smiled and punched me gently on the shoulder, but I knew she meant it. I let it drop.

It's funny now, but at the time I was disappointed and to be honest a bit confused. God had been growing this idea in me that He wanted us to go to West Virginia and start a boys' home. And we had been seeking Him together, asking what He had for us. He had opened the doors for us to become houseparents at Eagle Ranch in Atlanta.

We were getting to the do the work God had called us to do; we had a house full of young men we were teaching and supporting and loving, helping them to know God and become the young men He intended them to be. I loved every minute of it, but the seed had started to grow in me that we should be doing this in West Virginia.

But I couldn't go without Dawn. I knew that for sure. I needed a whole team around me, and Dawn was my first-string quarterback. Without her, I wasn't going anywhere.

It was fall, and our Eagle Ranch boys were just getting back into the routine of school. So we settled in too. *Here we go*, I thought, *another year.*

And for some reason, I decided to let the topic rest and let God bring it back up. It must have been God who kept my mouth shut because my normal approach would have been to wear Dawn down with rhetoric, like this was "God's will," and we needed to "move and get going" and "make this happen."

But I just shut up about it and resolved in my heart to not say a word. If God wanted us to move, then He would have to change her heart. I wasn't going to be able to do that.

Over the years, I have seen many men and women who have what they think is a vision and a passion from God to do something big and courageous for the kingdom, only to launch out against the advice and counsel and affirmation of the people closest to them. I have seen many marriages suffer because the husband or wife was convinced they needed to make a move, to do something different—find a new job or start a ministry—and the other was dead set against it. Husbands and wives need each other's full support when it comes to life-changing decisions.

We need to be optimistic and wise when advancing our steps into a calling on our lives. God knows who we are married to, and to be equally yoked on a life's venture is very important. Slow down and make sure you have thoroughly talked and prayed your decision through. Period.

When we launch into battle, we need to have people by our side who are convinced we are doing what God has called us to do. We need people who will remind us when we get discouraged, when we are afraid of the attacks and troubles that are bound to come, that we have been called by God and that He will see us through.

My discussion with Dawn reminded me a bit of a story found in 1 Samuel 14. The nation of Israel and the Philistines were locked in a pretty long and protracted war. There had been many battles, with neither side really gaining much of an advantage. The Israelites were not very well armed. For the most part, only King Saul and his son Jonathan had swords, and they were severely outnumbered.

At one point the Israelites and Philistines made camp opposite each other near a pass at a place called Michmash. The Philistines had "three thousand chariots, six thousand charioteers, and soldiers as numerous as the sand on the seashore" (1 Samuel 13:5). The Israelites, when they saw their situation, hid in caves and thickets, some even in cisterns, and some deserted, fleeing across the Jordan. Obviously, there was going to be a battle; it was just a question of who was going to strike first.

Somehow, in the face of insurmountable odds, Jonathan got it into his head that he should take his armor-bearer and attack the Philistine camp. So they climbed down into the ravine and then started to climb back up the other side.

As they did, Jonathan cast his vision to his faithful armor-bearer, to let him know what he thought God was calling him to do.

> Come, let's go over to the outpost of those uncircumcised men. Perhaps the LORD will act in our behalf. Nothing can hinder the LORD from saving, whether by many or by few.
>
> —1 Samuel 14:6

I wish I had been there to see the look on the armor-bearer's face when he heard the plan. He knew the danger, undoubtedly. He knew it was more than likely a suicide mission, but he also knew Jonathan was convinced of his calling from God. And I think Jonathan was asking this young man to affirm his calling. He doesn't phrase it as a question, but implicitly he is asking: what do you think? The armor-bearer replies, "Do all that you have in mind . . . Go ahead; I am with you heart and soul" (v. 7).

Now it is a matter of some conjecture as to what Jonathan would have done had the armor-bearer refused to affirm his vision of attacking the Philistines, but I think he would have reconsidered what he was about to do. You don't go headlong into the enemy camp without someone who is with you heart and soul. I believe God affirmed His calling on Jonathan through that courageous, faith-filled young man.

And I resolved that if Dawn wasn't with me in body, heart, and soul, then we would not go. And so, I waited.

That Christmas, we got word my family farm in West Virginia was available if we would like to use it for a little vacation. No one would be there, and we could have the whole place to ourselves. It had been an especially busy fall, and Dawn and I were both physically and emotionally exhausted. The thought of a week on a beautiful, quiet, isolated farm away from the chaos of Eagle Ranch and the boys was very appealing.

So we packed our bags, loaded the car, and turned north toward West Virginia.

We hadn't talked about the boys' home in months, and I kept my resolution of silence the entire trip. I don't know if she expected me to bring it up at some point, but I was as silent as a grave. We were going on vacation, and in a week we would be headed back to our home in Georgia. That's what I was thinking, and that is what I fully expected to happen.

GOD WAS STARTING TO DO SOMETHING THAT WOULD CHANGE OUR LIVES FOREVER. And that is, basically, what happened. But I didn't know, as we wound our way through the narrow, snow-covered mountains, that God was starting to do something that would change our lives forever.

When we arrived, the farm could not have been more picturesque. Nestled in a narrow hollow, the tiny farm house, barn, and surounding pastures were covered in a blanket of white snow. We inched our way up the icy drive, glad to be out of the car at last. Before long we were settled in, a roaring fire in the hearth, soup warming on the stove filling the kitchen with a mouth-watering aroma. I took in a deep breath, feeling refreshed and rejuvenated already. As we went to bed, we thanked God for the safe trip, the warm roof over our heads, full bellies, and some time together.

I woke early the next morning; the air in house was crisp and quiet. I started a fire and bundled up to head outside. I wanted to break up some of the ice on the road we hit coming in, and the morning air was cool and inviting.

Maybe an hour later, I stamped snow off my feet and came into the kitchen. I called for Dawn, but there was no answer. I happened to look out the window and a patch of red caught my eye. It was too far away to see clearly, so I pulled out my binoculars: down across the ravine up on the next hill, I could see Dawn in her bright red jacket. She was sitting, head bowed. It looked as if she was praying.

Several moments later, maybe an hour, I heard her coming in the kitchen door. She looked at me when she entered: her cheeks were flushed, her eyes red. She had been crying.

"We need to come to West Virginia," she said looking at me.

I was stunned and stood in silence for what must have been two minutes at least.

"Are you sure?" I asked in a tone that let her know she could be honest.

"I'm sure," she nodded. "God wants us here."

And then I knew. She was with me heart and soul.

God uses others to speak into our lives. There are also people who will speak against your vision. Surround yourself with godly counsel. When God puts a vision, a seed, in your heart to do something for the kingdom, He will, at the right time, bring people who will affirm that decision, people who will confirm your calling and tell you to do "all that you have in mind," like Jonathan's sword-bearer told him (v. 7).

And so it is an important question to ask as you consider the seed God plants in you: Are the people closest to you supportive of what you want to do? Do they have a peace about the direction you think God is leading you? Are they with you, heart and soul?

If not, then I think you should stop, pray, and seek wisdom from God. I would

STOP TALKING ABOUT IT, STOP TRYING TO CONVINCE PEOPLE THIS IS THE RIGHT WAY TO GO, AND LET GOD START TO WORK IN HIS OWN TIME AND HIS OWN WAY.

advise to let things marinate for a while. Stop talking about it, stop trying to convince people this is the right way to go, and let God start to work in His own time and His own way. You're going to need a team of people by your side, and you are going to need them to be all in with the vision God has for you.

During college, I was working at Fuddruckers making hamburgers. It didn't take too long for me to realize this was probably not a long-term career path. I heard from a friend that police work had the potential for a bit more excitement than a fry cook, so I figured I'd take a chance.

At this time in Georgia, there was an interesting policy in effect where you could be hired and start working as a police officer without first going to the Academy for training. The Police Department only required new officers to attend the Academy training sometime within the first year.

I was not aware of the aforementioned policy. I was hired, given a gun, badge, uniform, and baton, and I was assigned a training partner, Adam Geiger, who would watch out for me until I could arrange to go to the Academy for my formal training. Until then, I was to follow Adam, ride with Adam, do what Adam did, and do what Adam told me to do. Basically, I was Adam's shadow.

I have never felt so ill-equipped for anything in my whole life. I still smelled like well-cooked sirloin, and there I was in the front seat of a police cruiser going on patrol.

I'll never forget our first call. I had no idea what dispatch was saying over the radio—or to what Adam was responding—I had not yet been trained to understand police lingo, what they call "signals and ten-codes," but we ended up at an abandoned industrial complex.

"We got a call of an active burglar alarm," Adam told me as he pressed on the accelerator. "We're going to go check it out." I slouched down in my seat and prayed. I prayed it was only a cat or a harmless homeless man and not the Mob or a group of terrorists. In a matter of minutes, we pulled up to the site, a collection of warehouses encompassing maybe 20 to 30 acres. It was huge, with a ten-foot-high chain-link fence surrounding it. Adam hopped out and told me to follow; we were going to check if any holes had been cut or gates left open. In my opinion, it was much safer to be wherever Adam was than left alone. I hopped out and quickly fell in line.

A quick survey of the fence and gate showed nothing out of the ordinary. The air was silent and still. In the distance we could hear a dog faintly barking; a truck downshifted on the freeway miles away. We turned back toward the car when suddenly the night silence was broken by the sound of metal falling on concrete, like someone dropping a wrench in a garage.

We stopped dead in our tracks, looked at each other, and turned to look back through the fence we had just checked. We saw the top of a metal extension ladder appear out of a window in the warehouse, followed by rung after rung, until finally a man dressed in a black hoodie and cap appeared, temporarily lit up by the street lamp overhead. He was followed, ten seconds later, by a second man, also in black. This man was carrying a large, heavy bag that caused him to stagger awkwardly.

Once on the ground they ran for the fence. Immediately, Adam barked three quick ten-codes into his radio and bolted to intercept the burglars. "You take the one with the bag," he whispered urgently, hoping to keep an element of surprise. As he did he drew his gun.

I looked at him in disbelief. A week earlier I was serving hamburgers. Now I was about to be thrust into what I could only imagine would be an all-out gunfight. I was beyond unprepared for this, I thought to myself as I started to run into the shadows after Adam.

A few years later, when I got the green light from Dawn, reality started to set in: we were going to start a boys' home in West Virginia—or at least try—but I had no idea where to even begin. We were houseparents at Eagle Ranch and had some idea how things operated, but to launch a new home and an entirely new ministry in a different state was way beyond my expertise. I felt a little like a fry cook thrown onto the front lines of the police force. I had already done that, and I knew it wasn't a route I wanted to take again.

I didn't know what to do, so I started to pray. I *did* know how to do that. I prayed for a mentor—someone who could train me and teach me, who could walk through the steps with me and give me instruction and encouragement along the way. I didn't know anyone like that, but I prayed and waited to see what God would do.

The church Dawn and I attended was just outside Atlanta and was one of those places big enough a member could go unnoticed. And while I went almost every week, there was no reason—other than the fact that I am six-foot-five—that anyone should notice me.

And so I was very surprised when, one Sunday, a lead pastor approached me and asked if we could get coffee sometime. His name was Dan Reiland, and we had met but were not especially close, more acquaintances than friends. I was surprised at the offer but happy to accept, and we met a few days later.

"So tell me, Steve," Dan started as we sat down in a local coffee shop, "what is going on in your life?"

It was a pretty direct question and caught me a bit off guard, but I recovered and started to tell him about this vision I had for West Virginia and that Dawn and I felt like God was calling us to start a boys' home. "But I have no idea what I'm doing," I confessed. "I've been praying for someone to mentor me."

Dan sat back and smiled. "Well, it's funny you should say that, Steve. I've been praying that God would lead me to some men I could invite to be a part of a group I lead called Joshua's Men. It is a yearlong mentoring program. I felt like He wanted me to ask youto be a part of the group this year."

I know God's timing is perfect, but looking back I had no idea just how much I needed that group to help me get going in the right direction. For the next year, Dan lead seven of us through a series of discussions on topics ranging from leading at home to vision-casting to public speaking.

It was exactly what I needed.

I was now surrounded by a group of godly men who could help equip, challenge, and encourage me as we got ready to move to West

Virginia. We met month after month, and I felt God using these guys to refine my vision and plan. I soon learned my plan had some serious holes. One of the guys in the group was Norwood Davis, who later became the chief financial officer of 12Stone. He was the worst because he asked the hardest questions.

"What are the needs for a boys' home in West Virginia, Steve?"

"I don't know."

"You haven't done a needs assessment?"

"What's a needs assessment?"

"How are you going to raise money in one of the poorest states in the country during a recession?"

"I don't know. What's a recession?"

You get the idea. It went on like this for close to six months. They'd ask questions: I'd answer, "I don't know." I needed these guys badly, and Chestnut Mountain Ranch would have never happened without God bringing that group of men into my life to equip and encourage and challenge me. That year, Norwood and the others helped me formulate a full-on business plan, complete with a needs assessment and demographic research.

Chances are you will not be totally equipped or prepared for the task God has called you to at the very moment He calls you. But I believe He will bring people into your life to help get you ready, if you are willing to let them in.

While there's no foolproof method for finding a group like Joshua's Men for everyone, the best place to start is on your knees. I wanted God to bring me the right person or people to mentor and help equip me, and I didn't want my own personality or efforts to get in the way. The best way I knew to get out of the way was to simply pray and wait.

And once again, just like with Dawn, God moved in just the right time to bring me the right men. He was building a team around me, and I believe He will do the same for you if you give Him the space and time to do it.

King David was a man on a mission. He had been called by God to cleanse Israel from foreign gods and influences and to lead the people God loved back to Him. In many ways, David was the greatest king in the history of Israel. He drove out many of Israel's enemies, and under his leadership, the kingdom grew and flourished.

But David had his weak spots too. It is hard to say what happened exactly, but it seems David got distracted from his calling, and as a result he got caught up in some activities that would lead him astray.

> *In the spring, at the time when kings go off to war, David sent Joab out with the king's men and the whole Israelite army. They destroyed the Ammonites and besieged Rabbah. But David remained in Jerusalem. One evening David got up from his bed and walked around on the roof of the palace. From the roof he saw a woman bathing. The woman was very beautiful, and David sent someone to find out about her. The man said, "She is Bathsheba, the daughter of Eliam and the wife of Uriah the Hittite." Then David sent messengers to get her. She came up to him, and he slept with her.*
>
> *—2 Samuel 11:1–4*

Unfortunately, we all probably know Christian leaders who have succumbed to the same temptation. While no leader is or should be expected to be without flaws, there is a principle at play in the story of David that I think is key for any leader—he was alone and separated from his team when he should not have been.

The author takes special care to mention that David's failure occurred in the spring, "at the time when kings go off to war." David had been a warrior and a fighter his whole life: it is what God made him to do, and he had done it faithfully for many years. It's not clear why he decided to stay in Jerusalem that spring, but he did.

What is abundantly clear is David did not have anyone who questioned this decision, at least not that we know of. Joab, a close friend and trusted colleague, seems to have simply accepted his orders to lead the army in David's stead without so much as a question. It must have seemed out of the ordinary to him. Kings go to war in the spring; that was David's mission, his calling. I would think for him to stray from this practice would have raised some questions among his trusted associates.

But no one seems to have said anything. To be fair to Joab, perhaps he did. And maybe David ignored him or refused to listen. What we do know is David did not have someone in his life, at this point, who could speak truth or confront him when he was veering off course. I wonder, had his confidant Jonathan still been alive, if things might have turned out much differently.

Ultimately the situation goes from bad to worse. Bathsheba becomes pregnant, and in an effort to conceal what he has done, David calls her husband home from battle and urges him to sleep with his wife. When Uriah refuses—out of respect for the men he left at the battlefront—David conspires to have him killed. When the deed is done, he brings Bathsheba into the palace and marries her.

Failing to remain on mission, and without accountability and transparency, David quickly unravels. Once full of conviction and integrity, David is now an adulterer and murderer.

It is important to mention at this point that I do not believe the future of Israel hinged itself upon this one man. God, in His sovereignty, was wholly in control of the situation and was going to accomplish all He wanted through His chosen people. What was at stake, I believe, was David's role and part in that mission.

Every leader needs people around them to hold them accountable to the mission and with whom they can be transparent. Without those people, we run the risk not only of straying from our calling but also being disqualified to participate in what God is doing.

While I was at Eagle Ranch, I decided to take on a car restoration project with the boys in our home. I had an old Nova that we dragged into the driveway, and almost every evening after dinner, a few of the boys and I would head out to work on the engine or do some body work. It was a great time to bond and get our hands dirty. I have great memories from that summer.

One evening while we were working, a passing car stopped, and the two guys inside rolled down their windows; they were obviously taking a closer look at what we were doing. One of the gentlemen I had seen around Eagle Ranch many times, although I didn't know him well. His name was Paul Smith.

"Love what you guys are doing with that car," he said through the window.

The boys all said thanks, and I could see their chests puff up a bit with pride. Paul said he loved hot rods and would race them at a local track. He invited us to come watch some time. He didn't have to ask twice.

Over the next few months, Paul and I spent more and more time together. I told him about our plan and dream to move to West Virginia to start a boys' home similar to Eagle Ranch. Paul got very excited, and we talked for hours about the ins and outs of my plan. Paul was retired and spent his time volunteering, but he had been the president of Kroger's Atlanta division for two decades; I valued his sharp mind and wisdom.

I also admired his humility and openness. We talked about everything, and he told me about many of the lessons he had learned while leading the chain of grocery stores. One of the things he impressed upon me was the need for transparency in the organization. "People have to be open and honest," he told me. "You have to create that kind of environment for them. *You* have to be transparent and open first."

Paul taught me that the only way I was going to stay on course and pursue the mission I had been given was to have people in my life I could be open and honest with and who I knew would hold me accountable. After we moved to West Virginia, Paul continued to visit regularly and served as a sounding board for new ideas and, I think, kept an eye on me to make sure I was doing what I needed to be doing! And I am really grateful for that.

When we formed our first board of directors and started hiring staff, transparency and accountability were two of our highest priorities. As a result, both the board and staff are comprised of people I first consider friends. Our relationships go beyond the organizational workings of Chestnut Mountain Ranch. We know each other, and any of them can look me in the eye and tell me what they really think.

For us, transparency began with our finances. Jesus says, "For where your treasure is, there your heart will be also" (Luke 12:34). I believe this means that if you are fully transparent with your financial dealings, then that is a good indication you will be transparent in other areas in life as well. And I would go so far as to say that any organization that hides its financial records probably has other things hidden as well.

Sometimes God brings you a glass of water.

We had just bought the property, and I was working on the tractor for a good bit of the day. We were trying to get things cleaned up and cleared out enough to bring people down to see what we had. I remember it was really hot, and I was covered in dust and dirt. To be honest, I was exhausted and feeling a bit alone out there by myself.

Suddenly an old, beaten-up car, a huge plume of dust and dirt in its wake, barreled down the hollow toward me. I hopped off the tractor and was looking for a place to dive into the ditch if I needed to when the car slammed on its breaks and came to a skidding halt about ten feet away. Inside was an elderly woman. Her hair was gray and a bit disheveled, but her eyes were lit up like two tiny candles. She smiled warmly.

"Are you Steve Finn?" she asked.

Surprised, I replied, "I am," and tried to remember if we had met before.

"Oh good," she turned off the car but didn't get out. "I saw you on the news the other night, about what you're doing down here."

I looked at her blankly, still in a bit of shock and wondering what would happen next. I think my police training was kicking in a bit. She didn't seem to notice.

"Well, God told me to come down here to pray for you."

"For me?" I asked, even more surprised.

"You're Steve Finn, right?"

"Yes, ma'am."

"Well then, I'm prayin' for you!" And she did. I don't remember what she said or even how long she prayed, but I do remember the tremendous refreshment it brought me. God told this woman, somehow, some way, to get up and drive down some little valley and find a man she had never met. And she did it. And it was exactly what I needed at that moment.

That episode has shaped, in some ways, how we have built the ranch. I knew we were going to need a team of partners, people to volunteer, contributors to give financially, but that woman showed me God would give us exactly what we needed, exactly when we needed it: the right person at the right moment.

When Nehemiah went to rebuild the wall around Jerusalem, he needed two things: materials and labor. At first he didn't have either. God was going to have to build a team around him to help shoulder the load and carry the burden if anything was going to get done. And He did.

Artaxerxes, king of Babylon, stepped up in a big way. He noticed his cupbearer Nehemiah's downcast spirit and asked him what was going on. Nehemiah told him about the broken walls of Jerusalem and the burden he had to rebuild them. Surprisingly, the king not only gave him permission to go, but he also gave Nehemiah all the timber he would need to accomplish the task. Artaxerxes was a big piece to the puzzle. Nehemiah needed a generous man like the king behind him, but Artaxerxes was only the beginning.

Once Nehemiah got to Jerusalem, the wall was in worse shape than he expected. It was going to be a massive job, and he was going to need a lot of help, so Nehemiah called together the Israelites living in the city, including the priests, nobles, and officials. He told them how God had been gracious and he had displayed favor for the king of Babylon. And the people rallied around him: dozens of names are listed in Nehemiah 3, each person doing their little part, their section of the wall.

Eliashib the high priest and his fellow priests went to work and rebuilt the Sheep Gate. They dedicated it and set its

doors in place, building as far as the Tower of the Hundred,
which they dedicated, and as far as the Tower of Hananel.
The men of Jericho built the adjoining section, and Zakkur
son of Imri built next to them. The Fish Gate was rebuilt
by the sons of Hassenaah. They laid its beams and put its
doors and bolts and bars in place. Meremoth son of Uriah,
the son of Hakkoz, repaired the next section.

—*Nehemiah 3:1-4*

Lots of people, doing their part. Nehemiah needed a team to help him carry the burden of rebuilding Jerusalem and the name of God.

It would take several books to mention and thank everyone who has been a part of the team to bring Chestnut Mountain Ranch to where it is today. Over the last decade or so, thousands of volunteers have helped clean, clear, dig, build, and paint for tens of thousands of hours as we've built homes and schools for our boys. Thousands of people have given money: some very large gifts, some the little they could afford. I wish I could thank everyone who has joined the team.

How do you build a team like this? The Bible says that those who are faithful with a little will be entrusted with more. We tried to remember this when building the ranch, especially when it came to bringing on financial supporters and volunteers.

I know directors and founders of boys' homes and other non-profit organizations who will not take a meeting unless the potential exists for at least a six-figure gift. They reason their time is too valuable to waste on smaller donations. I understand their reasoning, but I think that practice can very likely undermine what God is trying to do. And who knows how He is going to deliver His blessing? It'll probably come in a very unexpected way, from a very unexpected source.

Remember the woman, who gave just two coins to the temple offertory? Jesus said she gave more than anyone else, more than the wealthy men who threw in large amounts (see Mark 12:41–44). I am not sure how the accountants among us reconcile that math, but in God's economy, that is how things work. And I'd hate to miss out on God's blessing because I misread someone.

What this means practically is that I never say no to anyone who wants to meet with me about Chestnut Mountain Ranch or who has just an hour or two to volunteer and help. I will visit the smallest church in the country (I think I've been there!), not because I am anticipating a large pay day but because I believe we need to include as many people as possible in the mission and vision of Chestnut Mountain Ranch.

There is an added benefit to including many people, to allowing anyone to shoulder the burden with their finances or as volunteers: it keeps me from thinking this is just mine and all about me. Thousands of people are invested in the ministry. It is not just me, and I certainly have not done all the work—not even close. There is no way I could have done this on my own, and the more volunteers and team members we have the more I am reminded this work truly is not my work—it is God's and His alone. We just get to come along for the ride.

TOOL NO. 4:
PATIENCE

I am 47 years old.

I only mention it because it has been about 35 years since those nights back in Georgia when my father would come into my room late at night, when we would talk and dream about building a boys' home someday back in West Virginia.

Thirty-five years. That's a long time. And a lot has happened in the years since my father passed away. I wandered through my teens and finally landed on the police force in my early twenties. Eleven years there, then a few years at Eagle Ranch before moving to West Virginia in 2005.

It has been a long road to get where we are today, and a major thing that I have learned through the process of following God is it requires a lot of patience. Thirty-five years. That's longer than some of you reading this book have been alive. That's more than two-thirds of my entire life.

One thing I am pretty confident of when it comes to God is that He is not usually in too much of a hurry. He left Israel in captivity in Egypt for 400 years, and then they wandered another 40 in the desert waiting to get into the Promised Land. God even took 40 years to get Moses ready. Moses spent those years watching after a flock of sheep for his father-in-law.

Jesus waited 30 years to start His ministry, and we have all been waiting close to 2,000 years for Him to come back for us. God is very patient, and while that can be incredibly frustrating for us who live in a culture consumed by instant gratification, it is a really good thing. God does things for a good reason and with good motive. My mom didn't let me drive until I was 17; I hated the waiting, but it really was in everyone's best interest—mine and the other cars and pedestrians who, in some way, trusted my parents to make good decisions about their son.

There are at least four benefits of developing patience that come to mind: patience builds trust in God, it cultivates faithfulness, it is an incubator for growing in peace, and it develops endurance. Each one of these character qualities is vital for anyone who is a part of the family of God and engaged in building His kingdom.

However you define patience, I think of it this way: waiting. We only need patience when we are waiting for something to happen— for God to move, for someone to come or do something for us. And for those of us God has wired with a more entrepreneurial spirit, the work of waiting is not something that comes very naturally. We tend to jump on opportunities. When we see an opening we barge through, guns blazing. Our greatest fear is that we might miss a chance to do something, and once missed we won't get another.

Remember the old saying, "Opportunity knocks but once"? With God, I am not so sure that is the case.

Remember Richard, the Bible college graduate I met while on the police force? He told me he was in Atlanta working with kids, and over the course of a couple months we became pretty good friends. I would often find my way down to his house, and we would sit and talk about God and life. I often shared with him about my dad and his dream to build a home for troubled boys.

"Steve," he said, one afternoon, "I really think you need to come see what we are doing in the city. I think God is calling you into youth ministry."

"I don't know," I replied, "I'm just not sure I'm ready." He smiled and nodded, and we both just sat in silence for a few minutes.

The rest of the day, I couldn't get that conversation out of my head. I wrestled with the thought of leaving my job and launching into the unknown. Maybe God sent this guy to get me going; maybe this was opportunity knocking. After a couple weeks, I decided to go back and take him up on his offer.

My heart raced as I drove slowly past overflowing dumpsters and run-down shanty houses to the end of the street. His trade-mark motorcycle wasn't in the driveway, and my heart sank a little. Maybe he wasn't home. I walked onto the porch and peered in the dusty window. I was surprised to see the house looked abandoned: a thick layer of dust covered the floors, papers and trash littered the living room and hallway. There was no furniture. It looked like no one had lived there in years.

I've missed my chance.

I went back a few times, but no one was ever there. And that feeling that I had blown it, ruined God's plan for my life, continued to grow. To be honest, I started to panic a bit. I felt like I was getting left behind and I needed to catch up. I had missed this opportunity, and therefore I needed to hustle to get back in front of things. I started thinking seminary might be a good choice.

SO I TOOK A DEEP BREATH AND WAITED. I reached out to one of my pastors, Chris Huff, and told him about what had happened. His words were very comforting. "Steve, don't go to seminary. Not that there's anything wrong with it, I just think you need to stay patient and wait. Keep doing what you're doing, and wait and watch. I think God will provide another opportunity for you. Just trust Him."

It was exactly what I needed to hear at the time. So I took a deep breath and waited.

During the long period of their enslavement in Egypt, the Israelites groaned out to God. God heard them and remembered His covenant with Abraham, with Isaac, and with Jacob. So God looked on the Israelites and was concerned about them. Forty years later, God met Moses the shepherd on Mount Horeb.

Fortunately for me, it was not quite that long. Following the advice of Chris Huff, I waited. Dawn and I kept serving, praying, watching, and waiting for God to open a door for us. And during that time we learned trust. Day after day, somehow, our trust grew. We believed more and more that God cared about the children of West Virginia and hadn't forgotten them or us. We believed more and more that He was good, and when the time was right, He would come to us again.

One year later, after feeling like I had blown my one good chance, we were moving in as houseparents at Eagle Ranch.

Hindsight is always 20/20, and it is easy to trust God after the fact. But I thank God for the year we had to wait. It forced us to trust God, to believe His intentions are good and true in spite of the seeming delays, detours, and waiting we had to go through. And that year was a time we could go back to and remember, when it seemed like things were not going as quickly as we hoped. We could recall how God, in His time, lead us in the right path, and we could trust Him to do the same now. We could be patient again.

There is some matter of debate as to how long it took Noah to build the ark: a lot of people estimate 120 years. Other folks put the number closer to 60 years. Does it matter? Probably not. But it does raise a significant point: it took a long time.

About the only thing I have committed to for 60 years are my wife (Lord willing) and eating. And breathing.

Everything else is up for discussion. I am kidding, of course, but thinking about how long Noah worked on that boat, when (some argue) it had never before even rained, is an extreme example of fortitude, commitment, and resolve. Patience par excellence.

What is even more remarkable is the size of the ark Noah built. It was about 450 feet long, 75 feet wide, and 45 feet high and was divided into three levels. To give you some perspective on just how big that is, it was taller than a three-story building and had a total deck area the size of 36 tennis courts (or 20 basketball courts). It was as long as a football field goal post to goal post and nearly as wide. It was big enough to contain 522 standard US railroadstock cars.

ONE OF THE MAJOR BENEFITS OF LEARNING AND PRACTICING PATIENCE IS THAT WAITING PROVIDES AN OPPORTUNITY FOR DEVELOPING FAITHFULNESS.

If you stood the ark up on its end, it would have been as tall as the Great Pyramid of Giza.

Now, that's a big boat. And the Bible tells us Noah basically only had his family, maybe eight people total, to help him build it.

It really is amazing that they could get it built, and I am sure it took every bit of 60 years to do it: one nail at a time, one board at a time. It took patience, perseverance, and discipline to get up every morning and get back out and build. It took a lot to build an ark that size, but more than anything it took faithfulness.

In my opinion, one of the major benefits of learning and practicing patience is that waiting provides an opportunity for developing faithfulness.

God gave Noah a directive: build an ark in anticipation of a much larger calling—I am going to destroy humanity and start over with you. This was a grand calling to be sure, but its fulfillment was a ways down the road. First, there was the more mundane, daily chore of building a very large boat. God could have easily given Noah a boat or provided another means of surviving the waters, as He did when the Israelites were escaping Pharaoh's charging chariots through the Red Sea. Imagine if God had asked them to make a boat for that.

But God gave Noah the task of first making an ark. I think it is because He wanted to develop and build some faithfulness in

Noah. *Here's a small task, now go to work on this for a few decades, and then we will get to the bigger stuff.*

Sometimes we get annoyed with this kind of teaching method. We would much rather jump right into the important matters, but God sees everything differently and understands the value of a season of faithfulness in the midst of waiting.

This process reminds me of Mr. Miyagi having Daniel wash all his cars and paint his fence for days and hours in *The Karate Kid* (the original, please). Daniel was frustrated because he wanted to learn karate, but wise old Miyagi was doing just that, repeating the same controlled hand motions over and over. Daniel just didn't know it.

God is way smarter than Miyagi, but He does the same thing: practice this little task, be faithful with that, and before you know it, bigger things will come your way. But you have to be faithful and patient with a little before you are given more. As Jesus said, "If you are faithful in little things, you will be faithful in large ones" (Luke 16:10 NLT).

One of the first donations we received after the purchase of the property was for a baseball field for the kids. At this point we didn't have much of the infrastructure in place: we did not have gas, water, or electricity. We needed to build roads and homes and an administration building.

We knew we eventually wanted to have one, but at the time, a baseball field was not our most pressing need. But that was what the money had been designated for, and so that is what it had to be used for. It was mid- to late summer, and the last thing I wanted to do was to climb on a tractor and start pushing dirt around. Unfortunately there was not much else going on. And I figured we had the money, so I better get to it.

WE HAVE ALL STOPPED TO ASK IF THE MUNDANE, DAILY THINGS THAT SEEM TO SAP OUR ENERGY AND STRENGTH MATTER AT ALL. WE ASK, "WHEN WILL I GET TO MOVE ON TO THE GOOD STUFF? WHEN DO I GET TO BEGIN THE IMPORTANT THINGS THAT GOD HAS CALLED ME TO?"

It was miserable work—dusty and dry and hot. I would climb down after eight hours on that machine caked and crusted with dirt. It was no ark, but it felt like it was going to take forever. I had a lot of dirt to move and trees to cut down and stumps to remove. Eventually, I got it all leveled out and then went to picking out rocks by hand—thousands would be a rough estimate.

More than once I thought, *What in the world am I doing out here?* I am supposed to be reaching kids and helping families, and here I am picking up rocks by myself for days on end. I wondered if Noah ever had one of those moments, covered in dust and gopher wood sawdust and maybe pine tar, if he just looked around and thought, *What in the world?*

The reality is that we've all had those moments. We have all stopped to ask if the mundane, daily things that seem to sap our energy and strength matter at all. We ask, "When will I get to move on to the good stuff? When do I get to begin the important things that God has called me to?"

Somewhere along the way it dawned on me that although building an ark and making a baseball field are not that glamorous, what they accomplished were to build in me (as with Noah) a faithfulness with small things that was going to be vital moving forward. I came to understand that most of what I was called to accomplish each day was going to seem insignificant at the moment, but in the end, over time, it would result in something huge and more than I could have imagined.

There is an old maxim that asks: how do you eat an elephant? The answer: one bite at a time. Waiting and seasons of practicing patience provide amazing opportunities for faithfulness, which in turn yield big results.

If Noah was faithful to build that ark one board at a time, then he could be trusted to save the whole of the human race. If I were faithful to use the money as it was intended, to build that baseball field—one stone, one seed of grass at a time—I would see God bring other, bigger gifts as well.

The funny thing is, both things happened. Noah saved humanity, and Chestnut Mountain Ranch saw more money come in. We now have a 225-acre campus, two miles of roads, an infrastructure, an administrative/counseling center, a school, two boys' homes, a baseball field, a basketball court, a pavilion, an animal barn, and staff housing. And more. Maybe because we built a baseball diamond.

It is pretty tempting to look and wish for shortcuts in order to get out of being patient. If we can get something done quickly, we think, that's the better route; it is more efficient. I've learned over the years that sometimes it is good to be patient; that there are some important lessons to be learned, like faithfulness; and even that it can be harmful, in the long run, for shortcuts to bail us out.

A few years ago, I was told one of our biggest donors passed away. Afterward we anticipated a very large gift, enough to effectively complete the construction we needed to do and move into full-on operational mode. But the gift never came. It is hard not to be a bit discouraged by this kind of news. One of my primary roles as director for Chestnut Mountain Ranch has been to raise the funds we need to finish construction and pay our operational costs. That gift would have made my life much easier.

Maybe I am just trying to put a positive spin on not getting the donation, but I really think God was protecting us a bit from all that cash. (I can't believe I am admitting this!) While it would

GOD CARES MORE ABOUT BUILDING PATIENCE AND FAITHFULNESS IN US THAN JUST PROVIDING SHORTCUTS AND QUICK FIXES. have been a huge blessing and really moved us forward, it would have also had some consequences. Namely, we—or more precisely, I—would not have had the opportunity to build and develop a solid, large donor-base through which hundreds or even thousands of people would faithfully pray and give to the ministry of Chestnut Mountain Ranch. We would not have learned to be faithful, daily reach out to people with our story and travel the dusty backroads to little country churches and women's books clubs.

The work would have been completed, Chestnut Mountain Ranch would have been built and operating, but at the expense of building that wide, day-after-day foundation of faithful stewardship and hard work that I think far outweighed the quick fix of an enormous gift.

God cares more about building patience and faithfulness in us than just providing shortcuts and quick fixes. He knows that's much better for everyone in the long run.

"Hey, Steve, you got a minute?"

It was Clay, Chestnut Mountain Ranch's program director. He had a piece of paper in his hand and a nervous look on his face.

"Yeah sure, what's up?" I said looking up from a stack of papers on my desk.

"Well, it's about the money," he said a bit sheepishly. He set the paper in front of me on the desk. "I don't think we're going to make payroll this month. It's just not there."

"Hmm," I said in a tone belying that slight twinge that had gripped my chest. "Let me take a look at that."

He was right, we were running short, which didn't make sense to me because it was closing in on the holidays, a time when money usually came in pretty well. I was confused, and my face probably showed it. Clay didn't say anything; he just stood in the doorway.

"OK, thanks," I finally said. "Let me think on this a bit." He closed the door. I could hear him walk away, his steps echoing in the empty foyer.

Over the years, I have learned there are basically two ways to respond in that kind of situation. The first is to call all your staff in to let them know the state-of-emergency and declare that from then until the foreseeable future it is "all hands on deck." That means we drop everything and singularly focus on the problem at hand (i.e., raise some money). Everyone is to scour and reach out to every last person who has ever even hinted at an interest in Chestnut Mountain Ranch—your mailman, pastor, mechanic, grandmother, and the guy you caught staring at your ranch T-shirt in the checkout lane at the grocery store.

In short, you enter into a season of a controlled panic. You put your nose to the grindstone, and you go nuts to fix the problem.

This is not a fun position to be in. The stress level is high, and it does not do well for one's ability to sleep, think, or relate to the people you love in any manner other than an occasional grunt or wave of the hand telling them to get away and stop bothering you.

Time is of the essence because payroll is coming, and people do not like for paychecks to be short or withheld altogether. This approach to funding shortages is what I call Panic Mode, and it is, quite frankly, the opposite of patience. And it's certainly the opposite of peaceful. It is all-out war. No one gets to sleep or relax or be happy during Panic Mode.

I TOLD THEM THAT INSTEAD OF DIGGING IN AND WORKING HARDER, TRYING OUR HARDEST TO GET THINGS MOVING AGAIN FINANCIALLY, WE WERE GOING TO UNPLUG AND SPEND MORE TIME IN THE WORD AND IN PRAYER. WE NEEDED TO DO THE OPPOSITE OF PANIC; WE NEEDED TO WAIT ON GOD. TO BE PATIENT.

When Clay delivered the news, I admit, as the guy whose job it is to bring in the resources for Chestnut Mountain Ranch, my first instinct was to go into full-on Panic Mode, but for some reason I didn't. Maybe I was feeling a bit more spiritual since we were near Christmas. Maybe I was tired from another long year. Maybe the Holy Spirit was telling me to try a different approach this time.

So I decided we needed to fast and pray for the next three days and wait to see what God would do. I called the staff together and apprised them of the situation and what I thought we should do. I told them that instead of digging in and working harder, trying our hardest to get things moving again financially, we were going to unplug and spend more time in the Word and in prayer. We needed to do the opposite of panic; we needed to wait on God. To be patient.

There is a marked difference between people who are patient and those who are not. I think it is fair to say that the former experience a pretty fare amount of peace regardless of the situation. The latter tend to experience more stress. Patience, waiting on God to act, is a great test and place for us to learn to be at peace in even the most trying times.

A couple examples from the Bible come to mind.

There is an account that appears in a couple of the Gospels in which Jesus and His disciples were crossing the Sea of Galilee when a massive storm hits (Mark 4:35–41). We know it must be pretty big because the disciples are freaking out, and they are experienced, professional fishermen. Jesus, on the other hand, is in the bow of the boat, sleeping like a baby.

The whole scene couldn't be a more vivid picture of contrasting reactions to trial. The disciples panic and rush to wake up Jesus, asking Him if He even cares if they drown. Jesus, on the other hand, seems to be at perfect peace, knowing (of course) that God (i.e., Himself) has everything under control.

It is hard to blame Peter and the gang. In the face of a veritable monsoon, it would have been tough to get some sleep and experience the kind of peace that Jesus had. I would have panicked too. But I guess if there is ever a place where you to really experience peace, it is during the time you are wondering if God will show up, crisis or not.

Remember the moment right before Jesus is arrested in the Garden of Gethsemane (John 18:1–11)? Peter is there, of course, and standing with Jesus as the troops approach to arrest his leader. We all know Peter is not one to really wait around for someone else to do something; he takes matters into his own hands, grabs a sword, and takes a swing at a servant's head, fortunately getting only his ear. Maybe Peter didn't panic. Maybe. But he certainly got a bit jumpy, and I don't think there is any way you could say he was in a peaceful state of mind. He was in a state of war.

Trials are going to come, and we are going to wonder if Jesus or God or anyone else is going to show up to do something. These can be tense moments full of panic and knee-jerk reactions, or they can be moments when we decide to trust, to believe God will arrive in time, and we can simply rest in that knowledge. I think we get to choose: panic or peace.

For three days we fasted. We slowed down, turned off our computers, let the phones ring. We prayed a lot more and read our Bibles. For a time, I forgot even what we were doing everything for because I was enjoying a tremendous measure of peace. I can't explain it really. Maybe this is what Paul was talking about when he wrote:

> *Do not be anxious about anything, but in every situation, by prayer and petition, with thanksgiving, present your requests to God. And the peace of God, which transcends all understanding, will guard your hearts and your minds in Christ Jesus.*
> *—Philippians 4:6–7*

The reality of the financial pinch had not gone away, but we had given the worry, the anxiety, and the panic to God. In its place we experienced incredible peace. We would not have had that peace had we not been patient, had we not trusted God and waited for Him to do His thing.

They say you are supposed to ease off a fast, to eat a few small meals and get your stomach used to having food in it again. We decided to take another approach and planned a huge lasagna dinner with breadsticks, salad, and cheesecake for dessert. We were hungry.

I prayed for the meal that night. We thanked God for all He had provided and would provide. I said "amen," and everyone reached for the nearest bowl, dish, or platter. I'm glad we didn't have any fake fruit on the table.

No more than five seconds after I finished praying for the meal, the phone rang. It was six o'clock on a Friday evening, and it was not a time we normally got calls. It was odd to say the least.

But as I said, we were hungry and had just started dinner, so I let it ring. Everyone else was face-deep in their plates. But the phone kept ringing. Finally, I thought I'd better answer—maybe something had happened to someone. I'd better check because people just don't call at that time of night. I made it to the office on about the tenth ring and picked up.

"Good evening," I said into the handset, "Chestnut Mountain Ranch, this is Steve. How can I help you?"

"Good evening," said a man's voice on the other end. "My wife and I have been following the ranch there in the news, and we just wanted to let you know that we've recently come into some money. I don't know why, but I felt compelled to call tonight and let you know we have a check here for you for $10,000."

Not much can shut me up, but I stood there for a full minute, dumbfounded. Plates and glasses were clinking in the other room. I could hear laughter and talking.

"You there?" the voice on the other end of the line asked.

"Yes sir, I'm here."

It is not easy waiting on God and being patient, especially in the face of a crisis. It is far easier to take the reins, try to control, and dig in. It is easy to go into Panic Mode. But for those who will trust God, for those who will wait, knowing that He will arrive in His time, I believe an incredible peace will come.

I hope as I continue to try to follow God, to trust Him in the storms that will come, I can remain patient and calm, and that I will abide by the words of the psalmist: "Be still, and know that I am God" (Psalm 46:10).

One day I was having lunch with one of the wealthiest men in West Virginia. We were talking about the future of Chestnut Mountain Ranch and the work and money that was still needed. He had been a very generous supporter and we had become good friends. We could talk honestly with one another. Finally, he asked me a question I get quite often from lots of people.

"Steve, why don't you just go to a bank, get a loan, get these houses built, and get on with the mission? You have the backing you need to do that."

It was a fair question.

I explained to him that we decided, before we had even moved to West Virginia, we would not take on any debt in the building of Chestnut Mountain Ranch. This was a policy we learned at Eagle Ranch, and I think it served us incredibly well over the years. We don't build or buy anything for which we do not already have the money in the bank.

To be sure, if we took out a loan we could get things built and done a lot faster. And this is exactly the point the donor was making. Why wait around for money to come in when kids and families so desperately need the services and help places like Chestnut Mountain Ranch are there to provide?

I think there are two key reasons a debt-free policy is beneficial. First, when you have debt, there is pressure from outside forces—banks and lenders—to make payments on the loan. It may seem trite, but I have seen how debt can really influence and dictate how an organization operates and the impact it can have upon its values. Debt, as the Bible tells us, puts us in servitude to those to whom we owe money. And that was simply not a position I ever wanted to put myself or Chestnut Mountain Ranch in.

The other reason we are debt-free is, perhaps, more compelling.

Adopting a debt-free policy allows God to dictate the pace of our organization, the pace of growth, the pace of expansion, and the pace at which we make decisions. When Dawn and I jumped into this adventure, we knew it would probably be for the rest of our lives and—Lord willing—would be more of marathon than a sprint. Now, I am no runner, but I do know that in order to complete a marathon, you cannot start off in an all-out sprint. There is no way you will make it the full 26 miles. You have to pace yourself.

Being debt-free is one of the ways we let God set the pace for our organization. If He doesn't bring in the money, then we accept that as either a closed door or that we need to exercise patience and wait on God to provide the needed funds. Waiting can be part of moving forward. Conversely, when the money is there for a given project, we know we can get going on the project without any reservation, hindrance, or second-guessing that we might be pushing too hard or fast in a direction God does not want us to go.

Maybe the bigger issue is this: If I were to compromise my values, our values, for the sake of moving the mission forward, then I am suddenly taking control away from God. And that is a bad place to be. We purposed that we would not take on debt to build Chestnut Mountain Ranch; to abandon that core value now would be to compromise my trust that God has called me to this ministry.

When the Israelites were taken captive by the Babylonians, Daniel was just a young man (Daniel 1:4–6). He was recruited by the Babylonian king to serve in the palace, and he quickly ascended to the top of the class. He was hardworking, principled, and intelligent; he also never forgot his God. He was disciplined and prayed three times a day without fail.

Daniel had no clear idea of how long Israel would be exiled in Babylon. He was waiting on God to rescue them, and all he had was an unwavering trust in God's timing and ability to provide for His people. Surviving in exile requires patience. Daniel survived for 70 years (Daniel 9:2).

While his character caused him to grow in favor and position with the king, it also gained him a few enemies. Eventually, some of the king's advisors hatched a plot that outlawed, under the penalty of death, prayer or worship of anyone other than the king of Babylon. When Daniel learned of the plot, he had a decision to make: compromise his values and stop praying or continue and trust God would show up and provide.

Daniel could have saved himself. He could have stopped praying to the God of Israel, but to do so would have been to abandon his core beliefs. Instead he waited on God. He let God determine his future instead of taking it into his own hands.

Here's how the story ends: Daniel is thrown into a pit of lions, much to the dismay of the king, who had been duped by his advisors all along. And God intervenes at just the right time. God closed the mouths of the hungry beasts and Daniel is saved, and so are his values. If Daniel had not waited but had taken things into his own hands, then he may have been spared. The results would have been much different though. More importantly, God would not have gotten the credit for the miraculous way He saved His servant.

I love it when we get to celebrate the way God shows up and provides in just the right way at just the right time.

Patience is a key tool, I believe, for anyone wanting to follow God's leading in his or her life. We are so anxious—so quick to make a huge impact—we rush out and do not consider the timing or pace God might have for us. We are in such a hurry to get things done that we neglect God's leading and desire to do things in His time.

So how do you develop patience? I don't know that there is a process for developing patience, but there are a few good questions to ask yourself to help discern whether or not you are being patient: Are you trusting God to bring opportunities for you, or are you forcing things? Do you feel stressed about "missed opportunities," or do you know that God will open the right door at the right time? Are you faithful with what God has placed in front of you today even if it may seem small or insignificant? Do you have a sense of peace about where God has you right now, or do you find yourself anxious and eager about getting going? Is there anything, any value, you are compromising to jump start your dream, or are you allowing God to set the pace? What values are you steadfast about that would allow God to control the rate at which you move forward?

Sometimes I feel like a kid in the back of the car, screaming every 15 minutes, "Are we there yet?" Patience is difficult to learn and practice, but we, as Christians, have the hope that God is near, He is not far off, and He knows the desires of our heart. He will come and lead us when the time is right. He won't wait forever. And I think we should be encouraged by that promise. As James writes:

> *Be patient, then, brothers and sisters, until the Lord's coming. See how the farmer waits for the land to yield its valuable crop, patiently waiting for the autumn and spring rains. You too, be patient and stand firm, because the Lord's coming is near.*
>
> *—James 5:7–8*

TOOL NO. 5:
DISCIPLINE

H ey, you!"

    I looked around to see where the voice was coming from. I stood in the middle of the hallway as hundreds of my high school classmates scrambled to get to class before the next bell. My eyes skimmed the swirling mass of humanity. It was easy to get lost in a school of 3,000 students.

"Hey, over here!" the voice called out again.

This time my eyes caught another set looking right at me. He was looking over the crowd too. About ten feet away, he smiled and waved for me to come over. He was older than most of the people in the hall, and I could tell by his warm-up jacket and sweatpants that he was a coach.

"Hi," he said as I slowly approached. "What's your name?"

"Steve." I replied cautiously. Even though I was big for my age, I was still a bit guarded in this new school. I didn't know too many people, and secretly I wondered if I was in trouble. I had not been doing too well since my father passed away a few years earlier. By default, I just assumed I'd done something wrong.

"Hey, Steve, nice to meet you," he smiled again, reaching out to shake my hand. I shook it cautiously.

What's this guy hiding? I thought to myself.

"Listen, we're having basketball tryouts soon. I wanted to invite you to come out."

"OK," I said before I realized the words were coming out of my mouth.

"Great!" he answered enthusiastically. "They're on Saturday. Main gym. 10 a.m. sharp."

"Thank you, sir," I replied.

"See you then," he slapped me on the back and was gone down the hallway, disappearing into the mass of students.

"See you then," I muttered almost to myself. I don't think he heard me.

Saturday morning my mother dropped me off outside the school. I held on to my duffle bag and stood on the sidewalk for a couple minutes before I went in. I was confident in my ability to play. I could handle the ball pretty well for a guy my size. I knew how to maneuver, box out, and rebound. I was a decent shot.

I took a deep breath and stepped through the double doors and into the gym.

There were about 40 boys trying out for the 15-man roster. It was a large school, and the talent level was impressive. But I believed I could compete if given a chance. We went through about 30 minutes of drills, passing, dribbling, shooting, rebounding, and defending before the coaches divided us up into teams of ten to scrimmage.

After a couple of uneventful trips up and the down the floor, I took my position in the center of the lane, looking to defend and get any rebounds that came my way. A shot went up and bounced to the weak side. One of my teammates grabbed it, and we started down the floor toward our goal.

To this day I am not sure what happened. All I know is that I took about two steps and then lost my balance. Most falls are less than graceful, and this is especially true for someone of my height. I staggered for what seemed like an eternity, trying to right the ship, but it was a lost cause. I put one hand to the floor, took another half step, but my momentum was too great and down I went, skidding, it felt like, on my face across the floor.

The rest of the team sped ahead of me while I tried to regroup as quickly as possible. I lumbered up and gathered momentum to run when the whistle blew.

"Someone get in for Finn!" I heard the coach yell. I stopped dead in my tracks and saw my replacement sprint to the floor. I shuffled off and stood on the sidelines waiting for my chance to get back in the game.

That chance never came. Tryouts ended an hour later, and the coaches let us know their choices. I didn't make the team. I was dejected and discouraged. I felt like I never had a chance; they hadn't really seen what I could do. They cut me loose after one day.

When I returned home that day, I walked through the garage to get into our house. I looked up and noticed the attic door open. I took the basketball from under my arm and tossed it violently into the opening in the ceiling. I never retrieved it. It is probably still there to this day. I was done. Done before I even started.

THERE ARE DISCIPLINES TO WHICH WE MUST COMMIT IF WE ARE GOING TO REACH OUR FULL SPIRITUAL POTENTIAL.

I often wonder what would have happened, what I could have achieved as a basketball player, if I had been given the chance to play and grow and practice on that team for more than one day. If I had persevered, practiced on my own, or maybe tried out for a city league team, there is little doubt in my mind I could have gone on to be a good ball player. One day wasn't going to be enough for me to realize my potential. I needed lots of practice, daily discipline, and work.

If we are going to be what God wants and calls us to be, it takes more than just a moment or two of effort. It takes sustained and committed, day-by-day discipline. If I was going to be a good basketball player, it would take more than one practice to get noticed.

There are disciplines to which we must commit if we are going to reach our full spiritual potential. And we have to do it day after day, year after year. Know your vision, and dig in. When you commit to the path God has laid before you, the real training begins. God will hone you and strengthen you. He will build grit in your soul, and create circumstances in your life that will cause you to rely on Him.

Now, of course it matters which disciplines you are committed to. Practicing my golf swing wasn't going to help me on the basketball court. I needed to be disciplined in the right things. For us to fulfill God's calling and potential, we have to commit to the right disciplines.

I think there is a real danger for those feeling called by God to be disciplined in the wrong things, and if we are not careful, we can get caught building something that more resembles "my kingdom" than God's kingdom. The disciplines I have in mind are those that keep us closely connected to God. We need those things in our lives as often as possible, and they take some work and dedication to achieve.

When I was in Joshua's Men back in Atlanta, one of the first books we read was Richard Foster's classic *Celebration of Discipline*. In the book, Foster outlines several different types of disciplines that help us stay connected to God and on track with what He has called us to do.

There are basically three kinds of disciplines: inward, which offer avenues for personal reflection and change; outward, which help prepare and equip us to make the world a better place; and finally, corporate, which bring us nearer to one another and God. As I read, I thought, *This is exactly what I'm trying to do with the ranch*. If I wanted to make the world a better place for young men and their families, I needed to get some discipline in me.

There are four types of disciplines within each of these groups— 12 total, but I want to focus on the few that made the most impact as I followed God's leading to start Chestnut Mountain Ranch. We'll talk about the inward disciplines of prayer and studying God's Word, the outward discipline of solitude, and the corporate discipline of celebration.

I have had to work at each of these on a daily basis over the years, and I know they have been indispensable in staying connected to God and realizing the full potential to which He has called me. If we don't build disciplines that really matters into our daily lives, then we will one day realize we have wasted our lives and the potential God has for each of us.

There are probably few people who understood the need to stay connected to God through prayer and study of Scripture (and even fasting!) like Daniel. As a prisoner in a foreign land, an exile of Israel in Babylon, the pressures to conform and abandon his beliefs and values were constant.

Right off the bat, Daniel and other young Israelites were conscripted into the king's court for training and offered the most luxurious meals. Daniel sensed the danger of such a reckless diet and instead requested to eat only vegetables and to drink only water. His discipline to fast from the poor diet paid dividends even after the first month. When the king called him in for an interview, he found Daniel and his friends "ten times better" than anyone else in his kingdom (Daniel 1:3–20).

Daniel was equally committed to daily prayer and the study of Scripture. He stopped three times a day to pray and ask for God's direction and help (6:10). He regularly searched God's Word for insights and help in understanding the time he and God's people were in (9:2).

And it is pretty obvious Daniel and his friends needed that daily discipline. Not only did it earn them the favor of the king, it protected them numerous times from different threats. Daniel was called in to interpret a dream for the king, under a strict penalty. The king told his magicians and sorcerers, "If you do not tell me what my dream was and interpret it, I will have you cut into pieces and your houses turned into piles of rubble" (2:5).

Daniel needed a serious connection to God to be able to handle the challenge of this situation, a connection that only came with daily time with God through prayer and His Word.

Not long after, three of Daniel's friends faced death if they did not kneel to a golden statue of the king. They refused, confident they would be rescued. But even if He didn't rescue them, they would not bow because they knew that God was jealous and wanted them to put no god before Him (see Daniel 3:1–30). You don't survive those trials without some serious foundation in understanding who God is.

Even when faced with death in the lion's den, Daniel kept praying (see Daniel 6:1–28). Daniel's disciplines became second nature within his life, and when death stared him in the face, he boldly prayed. I think he felt it would have been more ridiculous for him to stop his daily discipline of praying than to face angry lions.

Daniel lived in a strange and hostile world, and he knew that in order to survive, he needed to be connected to God in a supernatural way. He did that through prayer, fasting, and daily study of God's Word.

When my father was diagnosed with cancer, I noticed he really started to study God's Word and pray a lot more. It was as if his disease ignited in him a more tangible and urgent need to be connected with God, as if he needed God's presence even more during that time. Something about that impressed me, even at 12 years old. And years later, when I experienced my own season of turbulence and doubt about my future and direction, I turned to God in the only way I knew how. I was 21 when I started seriously reading and praying for the first time in my life.

I am not sure what happened during that time, but I realized that thoughts and doubts I'd held on to for years, thoughts that I couldn't succeed, I was not good enough, and no one could love me, were being replaced by the truth and power of God's Word.

THAT IS THE POWER OF LISTENING AND TALKING TO GOD; EVENTUALLY YOU START TO BELIEVE WHAT HE SAYS.

My understanding of myself and how God viewed me was starting to change.

It didn't happen overnight, but the more I read and prayed, the more I started to think differently about myself and God and what my life could be. It took time, but I stuck to it, day after day.

That is the power of listening and talking to God; eventually you start to believe what He says. It starts to sink in and it starts to build a new, better foundation from which we can pursue our calling and mission. The inward disciplines of prayer and study puts into our minds the right words, the right voices that will give us a foundation for staying connected to God during difficult and good times.

"You should quit."

Her words cut through the silence in her office like a knife. I stood in front of my sergeant's desk, not quite at full attention but unmoving, staring straight ahead. I had been on the force for less than a year. She repeated what she said to make sure I heard her.

"I think you should just give up. I don't think you have what it takes to be a police officer in this town."

"Ma'am?" I asked. I was confused but didn't want to be disrespectful. I didn't understand her opinion. Had I done something wrong? Did I have some glaring flaw that she—and maybe everyone else—saw that I didn't? I was hoping for some clarification, but regardless her words stung.

"You're just too nice. You have too much compassion. Seems like you care too much about people. You don't have the edge that it takes to be a good cop, and I think this city is going to eat you up. You'd be better off looking for something else."

"Yes, ma'am."

She sat in silence. I didn't move but kept looking at the wall behind her. It was covered in awards and medals from a long, successful career.

"Well," she continued curtly, "you have anything to say?"

"No, ma'am."

Those are tough words to hear, especially as a new officer, and from your boss. Fortunately, I had been pretty steady in the Word and prayer for quite a while at that point and I knew, without a doubt, that God had called me to be a police officer. I knew I was supposed to be there because I had some things I needed to learn, and God was going to use that time to prepare me for something He had for me in the future.

I decided I would listen to God rather than my sergeant.

Had I not been neck-deep in the discipline of studying God's Word and prayer, I am not sure I could have survived that encounter. I think I would have believed her opinions of me. As it stood I was pretty solid in knowing what God had to say about it all. We had been in pretty close daily contact for some time.

"You're not good enough."

"You're lazy."

"You're going to end up just like your father, a loser."

These are the words most of the boys who come to Chestnut Mountain Ranch have heard almost every day for their whole lives. It amazes me that any parent could hurl such abuse at young children, but it happens too often. And eventually, with repetition, they start to believe it.

Anyone would.

This is why is it so vital they start to have a new word in their lives every day. They need to hear again and again that they are loved, forgiven, and accepted by God and by others. They need to know God wants a relationship with them, so much so He paid the penalty for their sins through Jesus, and if they will believe, they can come into His family as new sons.

I think it takes time to start believing those messages. You have to hear them over and over again, and then watch as the seed starts to take root and begin to grow into something beautiful and productive.

The fact is, most of the boys at Chestnut Mountain Ranch have heard—unceasingly—that they are not good enough, that they will end up just like their deadbeat dads, that they will fail. So every day we spend time in God's Word rebuilding their view of themselves and of God. These boys desperately need God's Word to ground them for the future so that they can be all God intended them to be.

It is a discipline; they don't always want to do it. Likewise, I don't always want to open my Bible, close my door, stop to pray, and connect with God.

And we study and pray because we know without that daily, regular connection to God, we and our boys cannot become what God wants us to be.

Out of all the types of outward disciplines, solitude has probably been the most important discipline for me. Primarily, solitude freshens my perspective on our mission because it keeps me from staying knee-deep in the middle of all the calls, the problems, the noise, the stress, etc.

When I take time away from my ordinary responsibilities and environment, I get a different view and can often see things—important things—that I may have missed otherwise. Never stepping back from your work can be like going to a museum and sticking your face right up to the paintings. You see all the intricate and amazing details, the brush strokes, the layering, but if you never step back, you're in danger of missing the whole picture. Solitude gives me a chance to step back and look at the big picture, which is good for me and for Chestnut Mountain Ranch, not to mention my family and everyone else who works with me.

Solitude also creates more margin for God to take control. It reminds me that ultimately this whole thing is His anyway. I have to trust God to handle it.

I think self-starters and natural-born leaders have the most difficulty stepping away and letting someone else, much less an invisible God, run the show for a few days. None of us would admit it, of course, but more than likely that's what keeps us from the discipline of solitude. We're afraid of what might happen when we are gone. Do you know any leaders like that? Do you have bosses, colleagues, or ministry teammates who never take a vacation and are always on call? I'd say they lack the discipline of solitude.

It is a bit unfair to always compare how we lead with how Jesus led, but He at least sets a standard to which we can aspire. And He never did anything without a reason.

Have you noticed how, just when things start to heat up and lots of people are starting to follow Jesus and the ball is really rolling on this kingdom He is establishing, Jesus takes off, ditches the crowd, and disappears for a few days?

> *That evening after sunset the people brought to Jesus all the sick and demon-possessed. The whole town gathered*

at the door, and Jesus healed many who had various dis-
eases. He also drove out many demons, but he would not
let the demons speak because they knew who he was. Very
early in the morning, while it was still dark, Jesus got up,
left the house and went off to a solitary place, where he
prayed. Simon and his companions went to look for him,
and when they found him, they exclaimed: "Everyone is
looking for you!" Jesus replied, "Let us go somewhere else—
to the nearby villages—so I can preach there also. That is
why I have come."

—Mark 1:32–38

If you're like me—and thank goodness Jesus was not—then you would have run back to the town and all those supporters. Work to be done, lots of people to heal. But Jesus avoided that trap. He goes off by Himself and prayed, which I think helped Him stay focused on His mission. It kept Him centered on what He was doing. He had to keep preaching and not get hung up with the same people, the same routine of healing everyone. I'm speculating, but He may never have made it out of that first town if He hadn't left and gotten some solitude and spent some time away from the crowds.

And if we don't practice the discipline of solitude with some regularity, we may get stuck and lose our original mission and calling.

There are lots of other stories like this about Jesus in the Bible. The crowds swell, and He retreats to pray. Sometimes He takes His followers with Him; sometimes He goes alone. And sometimes He sends them away, letting them carry on with the work. It is a kind of solitude where He is absent, and the work of building the kingdom continues.

After this the Lord appointed seventy-two others and sent
them two by two ahead of him to every town and place
where he was about to go. He told them, "The harvest is

plentiful, but the workers are few. Ask the Lord of the harvest, therefore, to send out workers into his harvest field. Go! I am sending you out like lambs among wolves."
—Luke 10:1–3

It may seem a little weird to say, but I wonder if Jesus might have been nervous about doing this. But He entrusted the 72 to do work for Him and for the kingdom. They were going to prepare the way for Him, and while it doesn't say exactly what He was doing in the interim, Jesus was out of the picture for a few days. He had to let others, and more specifically His Father in heaven, take control of things.

Jesus doesn't have the same hang-ups we do about solitude, probably because He had a better foundation in the disciplines of prayer and fasting and studying the Word. Most leaders I know hate to pull away. It is a real struggle and takes a lot of discipline to do so with any regularity. But if we do, we will be reminded that our work really belongs to God and everything will be OK.

After we had been in West Virginia for about a year, Dawn and I were down to our last few hundred dollars. We had made a few contacts, but the all leads we had on land for the ranch had fallen through. West Virginia is mostly a rural state, and I knew it was important to find land somewhat close to a populated city that could offer educational and medical services. We focused in on the counties around the city of Morgantown. As we talked with one owner, the price of the land increased significantly by hundreds of thousands of dollars.

We were completely exhausted, emotionally and physically. Financially we were tapped. I remember thinking I just needed to get away.

I needed to clear my head. With all the pressure and obstacles we had on our plate, it wasn't an ideal time, but I did not really know what else to do.

So I took some time away for a little while. I focused on prayer, solitude, and studying God's Word. I knew I needed Him then more than ever. The vision to start a home for children was at a fragile stage, and if things didn't change quickly, it was over. It looked as if we would have to go back to Atlanta. I was already reviewing job applications for the police force.

OUR CALLING IS ULTIMATELY HIS RESPONSI- BILITY. WE JUST GET TO BE A PART OF IT.

After that time away, all I remember is an incredible peace that everything would be alright Somehow, in the solitude, I was able to hear that quiet reassurance from God.

A few weeks passed. God was working on me at a new level. He had me right where He wanted me. Then came a call about another possible location. Within a couple months, we had our land, an even better parcel than what we had been trying to buy from the other guy.

As leaders, we are a passionate and committed people, and it is against our nature to disengage, even for a short period of time. But if we will, we can gain not only perspective and insight but also grow in our trust that God is in control and our calling is ultimately His responsibility. We just get to be a part of it.

I am not really an extrovert. Dawn and I don't go out too much, except maybe for dinner with friends from time to time. But we do like to celebrate, especially what God has done as we have stepped out to follow what we believed to be His call on our lives.

When God needs to get our attention and teach us new levels of discipline, He will orchestrate events to take us deeper. It is interesting to me that Foster's book lists celebration as one of the corporate disciplines, only because it seems to me that being thankful and grateful should come pretty naturally to us.

But often we forget to be thankful, or worse, we don't thank the right people. When I was young, my mom would have to remind me to write thank-you cards for gifts received, and it is no different with my own children.

Celebration is an important discipline for any leader for two reasons. First, it builds a foundation for future growth and stability. Second, it keeps us humble, acknowledging what God has done and not us, which is the most important aspect of any discipline. It keeps us from thinking too highly of ourselves.

King Nebuchadnezzar was a powerful man, and one night he had a dream he saw a great and mighty tree. It grew large and strong so that its tips touched the sky, and it could be seen from the ends of the earth. Its leaves were beautiful, and it had plenty of fruit to feed everyone.

Unfortunately for the tree, a messenger came down from heaven and ordered it be stripped of its branches. Its leaves and fruit scattered, leaving only the stump and roots to be bound by iron and bronze and to dwell with the animals.

The king was nervous about this dream and called for Daniel to interpret it. The dream was indeed about the king, and unless he renounced his sin and wickedness and acknowledged that heaven reigned, he would end up like the tree (Daniel 4:4–27).

The king didn't acknowledge the reign and supremacy and blessing of heaven (i.e., God, in all His accomplishments). It took a year, but eventually that attitude caught up with him:

> Twelve months later, as the king was walking on the roof
> of his royal palace of Babylon, he said, "Is not this the

great Babylon I have built as the royal residence, by my mighty power and for the glory of my majesty?" Even as the words were on his lips, a voice came from heaven, "This is what is decreed for you, King Nebuchadnezzar: Your royal authority has been taken from you. You will be driven away from people and will live with the wild animals; you will eat grass like the ox. Seven times will pass by for you until you acknowledge that the Most High is sovereign over the kingdoms on earth and gives them to anyone he wishes."

—vv. 29–32

The discipline of celebration helps create a habit of acknowledging the goodness and greatness of God. Nebuchadnezzar had that chance, he was even warned of what would happen if he didn't give credit to God, and he suffered the consequences.

Now, I am not saying that if you don't celebrate and give God the credit, you are going to end up a crazy person eating grass in the field for seven years, but it is not without precedent. If we refuse to humble ourselves and acknowledge and thank and celebrate what God has done, God has amazing and effective ways of humbling us Himself.

And besides, there really is something more gratifying and just plain ol' fun about celebrating someone outside ourselves. Some people really long for the spotlight, but it is the mature parent or friend who understands that real joy and happiness and excitement comes when we celebrate the greatness of others.

Celebrating what God has done is somehow sweeter than taking credit ourselves. The vision you have is His vision, and you are a part of His story. Do not forget this. We bless God and He blesses us. Avoid pride at all cost. Embrace humility, and stay open to His next directive for this journey you are on. His blessings may come in the form of financial gifts, but He may also bless you with lessons you need to learn through lean times. I have experienced a deeper focus and experience with God when I needed Him the most, and trust me when I say these seasons are truly a blessing.

However, it is a discipline. We have to work at it because giving credit to others or to God does not always come naturally. This is probably why Paul encouraged the Philippians, "Rejoice in the Lord always. I will say it again: Rejoice!" (Philippians 4:4).

Likewise, God ordained certain feasts and celebrations to be carried out on a yearly basis by his people Israel to remind them to celebrate. Passover was a time for them to remember how God rescued them from hundreds of years of slavery in Egypt. The Feast of the First Fruits celebrated God's bounty and generosity in the Promised Land. The Feast of Tabernacles celebrated God's presence with His people and looked forward to the coming Messiah. And there were more celebrated every year, so the people would not forget the goodness of God and start to think too highly of themselves.

The property we finally purchased for Chestnut Mountain Ranch ended up being the best piece of land and price of all the options we considered—it was exactly what and where God intended. It was closer to town and fit our needs perfectly. The only problem was that the price was still more than $700K, and we had hardly any savings in the bank. The owner had other offers, yet he was the first to embrace our vision, and he allowed us nine weeks to see if God was in this ministry with us.

We couldn't go to a bank for a loan because we had committed to being debt-free. In just weeks we had to raise everything, all

$700K-plus. I felt a little like Moses standing in front of the Red Sea. We had made progress, but now what? How in the world would we get through this?

That period of time was a blur of activity: phones calls, meetings, speaking engagements, and newsletters. It was an impossible task to raise such a large sum of money, but we knew God could do it if He wanted to. We never doubted and simply did our best to work hard and see where we landed in nine weeks.

I'd like to think I know a little bit about how Moses felt when the waters started to part in front of him. It is indescribable to see God work in miraculous ways. To this day, I do not know how it happened, but in nine weeks, we saw close to $720K come in for the land. My hand shook as I wrote that check and moments later, when I handed it off, I wondered if I had just done the stupidest thing in my life. We were back down to $400 in our account.

But God had done it, and I knew He could do it again. And we celebrated. For weeks, all we could talk about was how God had brought the right people at the right time to meet the need we had. Many nights I would lay in my bed, look at the ceiling, and thank God and marvel at how wonderful He was. I celebrated Him.

We still think about that season many years later. We still wonder and marvel at what God has done. And as we have talked about it over the years, each time thanking God for what He did, I think our discipline to do that has forged something in us: namely, an assurance and an increase in faith that God will continue to provide for us.

That's why celebration is so important: it sets a foundation for our faith and reinforces trust in God. We celebrate and acknowledge what He has done, and it builds a memory bank, a repository of understanding God's faithfulness from which we can draw when times get a little tougher and leaner.

The Israelites saw God do some awesome things—He provided protection and food and a new life of freedom. But when they forgot to thank God, when they grumbled and complained, it eroded their trust and faith in Him.

The discipline of celebration, remembering the goodness of God, gives us hope and faith during trying and difficult times. And that is a good reason to celebrate.

The inward disciplines of prayer and study put into our minds the right words, the right voices, that establish a foundation for staying connected to God during difficult and even good times. The outward discipline of solitude reverts our attempts at control back to God and reminds us that this whole thing is ultimately His anyway. And the corporate discipline of celebration builds a foundation for future growth and stability; it also keeps us humble.

But how do we develop discipline? I am not sure there is any easy answer to this, but three things have helped me build these disciplines in my life: commit, schedule, and start small.

I think commitment is, first and foremost, a mindset. Commitment happens when a person determines in his or her mind that he or she is going to do something, no matter what, even when the going gets tough. The committed person thinks and accepts this fate even before he or she has begun. Psalm 15 has been incredibly helpful for me in this regard:

> O LORD, who may abide in Your tent? Who may dwell on Your holy hill? He who walks with integrity, and works righteousness, and speaks truth in his heart. He does not slander with his tongue, nor does evil to his neighbor, nor takes up a reproach against his friend; in whose eyes a reprobate is despised, but who honors those who fear the LORD; He swears to his own hurt and does not change.
> —Psalm 15:1–4 NASB

Specific things jump out at me in this passage: the psalmist speaks truth in his heart, swears to his own hurt, and does not change. This is the person who connects with God. This is what it takes, I think, to walk with integrity and discipline.

I often remind myself of these verses when I want to skip time with God or not be disciplined about something: a righteous man speaks truth in his heart, swears to his own hurt, and does not change. That kind of mentality develops discipline.

It is helpful to schedule discipline into your life: daily, weekly, monthly, quarterly. However often you want or can practice discipline is up to you, but if it is not on the calendar, part of your to-do list, then it may not get done, at least not with regularity. If something is important, make it a priority and put it on your schedule. You manage to eat every day; there's no reason you can't schedule some time with God.

I think part of scheduling these disciplines is finding a place. I have several secluded spots around Chestnut Mountain Ranch where I can get away. I have my times in the Word in my kitchen or after I drive my truck to the top of a hill. You may have a favorite park or room in your house. Think through a few options that might work for you.

Finally, I think it is important to start small. I had a friend who decided the day before a race that he was going to run a half marathon. He thought he could just hop in and run 13.1 miles. Needless to say, it did not go well for him. He never ran again after that.

It takes time to build the muscle and endurance needed for some of these disciplines. Don't expect to pray for an hour your first day. It won't happen. Start by praying for five minutes. You'll probably really enjoy it and look forward to praying the next day. Eventually you'll pray more often and with more regularity.

Read for ten minutes a day for the first week, then see where it goes from there. If you struggle through an hour of study on day one, you most likely won't make it to day two. If you hike out in the woods to get away like a hermit for a week your first time seeking solitude, you'll probably feel like you're going crazy. Instead, take a 30-minute walk in the woods, and practice solitude sitting under a tree.

Disciplines are difficult; they may not be fun. And I guess the old saying holds true: if it were easy, then everyone would do it. But they don't, and I think that is why a lot of godly men and women get off track and lose heart following what may be very real callings in their life.

I hope you and I do not join them.

TOOL NO. 6:
PERSEVERANCE

Six months in prison.

I rubbed my eyes and blinked three or four times to make sure my vision was clear. I looked back at the piece of paper in my hand. The letter from the attorney general's office had just arrived at Chestnut Mountain Ranch. I could feel my pulse quicken.

I knew there were some people in our state who were not thrilled about us starting a Christian boys' home, but I never thought that what we were doing was illegal or that I would be facing jail time.

But the facts were in black and white. To be honest I was not really sure what we were going to do, but going to jail did not seem like a good option. And I think Dawn would have agreed with me on that one.

Perseverance is the ability to continue and not give up, even in the face of extreme and sometimes persistent opposition. Opposition can come in all sorts of forms and shapes, and we have experienced our share over the years. But we had a season right after we purchased our land that we came under what I can only call consistent and determined opposition from our state government.

We were gaining a little recognition from our local press as the idea of a boys' home in north central West Virginia started to take hold. There was no doubt the need in the area was great: everyone knew that school dropout rates were high. West Virginia also ranked high (or low, I guess, depending on how you look at it) in teenage crime, unplanned pregnancy, and drug use, so we were starting to gain some community support.

And so were various state agencies that, I assume, felt like we were stepping on their toes. Our first indication of this came in the form of a state law that was passed really before we even got going. While we had bought the land, we had no buildings, no children. We were not operational at all. But that did not stop this 76-page law from being passed in our state legislature.

We received a copy of this law, hand delivered to us, soon after the bill went into effect.

The letter informed us that Chestnut Mountain Ranch was under the jurisdiction of the state and as such was required to abide by the articles of the newly passed law. I won't go into all 76 pages of it, but the crux is this: any religious activity had to be completely voluntary and also allow for any student at Chestnut Mountain Ranch to choose an alternate activity. If we prayed for a meal, the kids had to sign a waiver that they had agreed to participate, and we had to provide them something else to do during that time, outside the premises, in an alternate location, if they did not.

In short, the law was so restrictive we would have essentially had to abandon our entire mission of introducing children to Jesus and raising them in a positive, Christian environment. This law was gutting everything we were trying to do.

I am a simple cop from Atlanta, not a legislator nor a lawyer. I do not have the experience or money to fight a state government. Honestly, I thought we might be done. I had no idea how to get a state law changed.

It is very likely that, as you follow God's calling on your life, there is going to come some opposition from the outside. Some person, agency, or organization might possibly rise up and try to stop what you are doing.

That is a surprising and bad day. It's surprising because it is hard to imagine anyone not absolutely loving you *and* your vision—I mean, you love you and your vision. It is bad because you realize things are about to get a lot more difficult. An obstacle, perhaps a very large one, is going to have to be overcome, and chances are it will require some sustained effort: in short, perseverance.

When Nehemiah went to rebuild the wall around Jerusalem, he had to be pretty excited that not only was he able to win the favor of the king but also of the inhabitants still in the city, those who had escaped the exile.

But his good vibes didn't last too long. Soon after construction was under way, word got out to neighboring kings and power brokers what Nehemiah and his crew were up to. People felt threatened; they were concerned he had designs on taking over the region, perhaps ousting them. He was a threat, and they were going to take him down.

In Nehemiah 4 we read that when Sanballat—whose name means "strength," by the way—heard about the rebuilding of the wall, he was furious. And his reaction was twofold: first he mocked Nehemiah, saying his work was shoddy and that if even a fox jumped on the wall it would fall down. I guess in those days this was considered a pretty good insult.

But then he got serious, and he rallied some other folks—the Arabs, Ammonites, and Ashdodites—and they conspired together to fight against Jerusalem and to "cause a disturbance in it" (Nehemiah 4:8 NASB).

One of my father's favorite books was Eddie Rickenbacker's 1967 autobiography. Many people have never heard of him, but he was one of America's first and best pilots during the First World War. Later, he founded Eastern Airlines and then was instrumental in World War II, serving as a consultant for Allied Forces.

During a mission to deliver a top-secret message to General MacArthur, Rickenbacker's plane went down. He and seven others survived the crash, and all but one managed to survive for more than three weeks on the ocean before being rescued.

My dad loved this story, and he shared it with me. And as I read it, I was inspired by these men's bravery and tenacity to hang on to life in spite of overwhelming odds. They were lost in the middle of an enormous ocean. No one knew where they were. They had very little food and next to no water, and several of them were quite injured.

And yet the persevered.

Rickenbacker recalls in his book the different methods he would use to keep his comrades from giving up. To some he spoke gentle words of encouragement. Others required Rickenbacker to yell and scream, to insight within them a will to fight, not just him but death.

As they struggled with acute thirst and hunger, Rickenbacker diverted their talk to God: twice a day they had "chapel." They would read from a little New Testament one of the guys had, and they would sing, sometimes just a few lines of hymns.

Every day, twice a day, and when their spirits and courage failed, Rickenbacker would implore them to fight and to hang on; surely they would be rescued, if only they could hold on for a little while longer.

Rickenbacker recounts how those times with God uplifted their spirits, encouraged them to hold fast. Even in the hardest of times, when things looked the bleakest, they believed their cries to God had not gone unheard and would be answered if they could only hold on for another day.

One of their favorite passages was Matthew 6, in which Jesus tells us not to worry about food or clothing but to seek first His kingdom. These verses encouraged the men to hang on, one day at a time, and to withstand the tremendous physical, psychological, and emotional trauma during those days at sea. Eventually, they were rescued.

There is going to come a time for anyone following the call of God when you are going to want to quit, pull up stakes, and go home. There will be times of loneliness and discouragement, times when you question God's call on your life, when you will be battered and beaten by others trying to destroy or frustrate or take over your work.

PERSEVERANCE IS A TOOL EVERY CHRISTIAN AND EVERYONE WITH A VISION AND MISSION FOR THEIR LIFE NEEDS.

Many people start out on a journey, born of God, and when hardship and trials hit, they fold, quit, and go home. They do not persevere, and therefore they miss out on the great adventure God has for them. Perseverance is a tool every Christian and everyone with a vision and mission for their life needs.

When my dad told me the story of Eddie Rickenbacker lost at sea, it stuck in my mind. His endurance in the face of great hardship inspired me. I knew that whatever happened, God had called me to start a boys' ministry in West Virginia, and I was going to persevere to the end.

If I am completely honest, there have been many days I would have been just as happy to go back to being a cop. I don't know how many times I wanted to pull up and quit after moving to West Virginia and starting Chestnut Mountain Ranch, but it was more than once. I have been discouraged, beaten down, tired, drained, confused, lacked direction, and felt entirely alone. During those times I would often think of the story of Rickenbacker and the men on those three rafts, and I would think, *No, I can do it one day at a time.*

In 1 Kings there is a story of Elijah, a prophet of God who spent a good deal of his career fighting against corruption and evil in Israel. There were not many people in his day who feared God, and Elijah was often left on his own to defend God's honor. Perhaps his greatest victory came at Mount Carmel, when he called fire down upon a few hundred prophets of Baal in what must have been an amazing confrontation. Elijah against the masses—well, Elijah and God.

Elijah's reward for his heroism in the face of intense opposition and danger? A death sentence from the evil Queen Jezebel. Only moments removed from an impressive victory, Elijah was on the run. And he ended up 90 miles to the south in Jezreel.

Not long after Elijah arrived, he got a message from Ahab, Jezebel's husband, that Ahab was coming to kill him. He had not run far enough, so he ran another day into the desert and finally stopped and sat down under a tree. And this is what he said to God: "I have had enough, LORD . . . Take my life" (1 Kings 19:4). He was exhausted, discouraged, and completely worn out. He fell asleep with these words on his lips, and I cannot say I wouldn't have done the same were I in his shoes.

But when he awoke, he was met with a surprise. An angel touched him and told him to get up and eat a small cake baked on hot coals and drink a jar of water. He fell asleep again. And again the angel woke him and told him, "Get up and eat, for the journey is too much for you" (v. 7).

What happened next is incredible: "Strengthened by that food, he traveled forty days and forty nights until he reached Horeb, the mountain of God" (v. 8).

I am not sure how up you are on your Middle East geography, but a direct route would be another 190 to 200 miles, or as far as 400-plus miles on published roads. Elijah ran for a month, plus another ten days. I don't care who you are, that's a long run. That is endurance and perseverance, right when he was ready to give up.

It is a mistake to think that we muster enough courage and strength on our own to persevere in the calling God has on our lives. I fully believe that God strengthens, empowers, and helps us when we have had enough. But make no mistake, the journey is going to be long, hard, and painful at times. Yet, God wants us to get up and run and run and run.

The good news is He is going to strengthen, encourage, and help us get there, every step of the way.

I think there are a lot of different kinds of obstacles that we have to overcome and trials we have to persevere through, so don't think this is a comprehensive list, but I want to share some of the trials and seasons I feel God called me to endure, to keep going in spite of the difficulties and trials that lay ahead. None of these were easy situations, and I'd be lying if I said there weren't times I wanted to quit. But by God's grace, help, and encouragement, we have made it through, and now we are stronger, hardened, and able to endure even more having been through these tough times.

I think the effect will be the same for you.

Not long after we received notice of the new law, we were contacted by the fire marshal informing us we would have to install specialized sprinkler systems throughout the entire property. I researched the cost and only found one other institution, in Florida, that had to do this, and it had cost them in excess of $3 million. That was going to be a real problem.

I could feel the armies drawing in around us.

It is tempting in those moments to think the task is too much, there is no way we could survive, and we might as well throw in the towel. We could not sustain all these attacks from powerful sources, it just seemed impossible.

There is an interesting passage in Hebrews where the writer is talking about perseverance. He writes, "You have not yet resisted to the point of shedding your blood" (Hebrews 12:4). Now he was talking about our struggle against sin, but I think the principle applies in cases when we feel overwhelmed. We haven't yet resisted to the point of shedding blood.

I think that is pretty descriptive language—and challenging. Yes, we were getting some threatening calls and letters from some powerful people. But we hadn't started to bleed yet. How could we even think about giving up so soon?

Nehemiah had just started to build the wall. He hadn't even been attacked yet. No blood had been spilt. And was he just going to fold and go home with his tail between his legs?

We get assaulted by sin. It pounds us from every angle every day. Are we going to give in or are we going to resist, maybe shed a little blood? And when we faced opposition from outside forces, we had to decide if we were going to give up, or were we going to persevere and resist?

We resisted.

And I am amazed, honestly, at how God provided the resources and people we needed to fend off each of these attacks. In two of the situations, influential men made phone calls to state offices and spoke on behalf of Chestnut Mountain Ranch and what we were doing.

I am sure other attacks will come. That is the nature of following the call of God. There will be obstacles, and the key is to be able to say you will not give up, you will resist, you will persevere to the point not only of shedding blood but even to the end of your own life.

It may come to that.

While you are almost guaranteed to have opposition from external forces that will require a good deal of perseverance and fortitude, chances are high you will have some internal conflict as well that will have you pulling out your hair.

In some ways, internal conflict can be even more difficult and painful to handle and requires even more courage and patience. You don't really expect friends and colleagues, those on your team, to get in the way. Internal opposition feels very much like betrayal, and it can take a lot to make it through that.

The Bible is full of people who had to persevere through opposition from their own camp, Jesus being perhaps the most obvious example. And I suppose, since He had to press on through Judas and Peter and truly the whole nation of Israel, His chosen people, then I suppose it should come as no surprise that we probably will as well.

For some reason I can especially relate to David. Here was a guy who did nothing but bail out Israel and their king, Saul, time after time, and how was he paid in return? He spent a good many years, four in total, running for his life. Saul had launched spears and armies to try and kill David (see 1 Samuel 18). Read through the Psalms sometime, and you will get a sense of just how difficult this season was in his life.

But maybe a lesser-known story about David comes later in his life after Saul dies a rather ignoble death in battle and David assumes the throne he had been promised as a child. David had a boatload of wives and quite a few kids, so it makes sense that one or two would go off the rails a bit.

But few of his children went to the extremes of his son Absalom.

In 2 Samuel 15 and following, Absalom set up a tent outside the city and basically told people going in to see his father that David was busy and wouldn't have time for them, but he'd be happy to help them with whatever they needed. If anyone would try to bow down to him out of respect, he would grab them and shake hands and not let them do it. The story goes: "Absalom behaved in this way toward all of the Israelites who came to the king asking for justice, and so he stole the hearts of the men of Israel" (v. 6).

He kept this up for four years, and then he made his move for the throne, declaring himself the king of Hebron, not long after David fled Jerusalem fearing for his life. It is a bad scene, and David apparently did not see it coming at all.

Absalom moved quickly to replace his father as the leader of all Israel, gathering support and securing allegiances from various advisors, one of whom suggested he should sleep with all his father's concubines as a demonstration of his power and contempt for his dad. It worked. The people fell right in line with Absalom, and soon he had David on the run with few remaining loyal to him.

David was no stranger to treachery and the pain of a friend that had become an enemy. Years of fleeing Saul had perhaps prepared him for this conflict with his son, but there can be no doubt that this betrayal affected him deeply. I am sure he grew tired and looked for some relief. Psalm 3 is a record of his thoughts as he flees his son:

> LORD, how many are my foes! How many rise up against me! Many are saying of me, "God will not deliver him." But you, LORD, are a shield around me, my glory, the One who lifts my head high. I call out to the LORD, and he answers me from his holy mountain. I lie down and sleep; I wake again, because the LORD sustains me. I will not fear though tens of thousands assail me on every side.
>
> —Psalm 3:1–6

It is one thing to persevere when the shots are coming from the outside. It is a whole other story to hang in and trust God when you are under friendly fire. I love what David says in this psalm: "I wake again, because the LORD sustains me." I can get out of bed today because God is giving me the strength. One more day—today—I will get up because God "sustains me."

"Steve, we need to take a vote."

I scratched my head, hardly believing what I was hearing.

"We need you to leave the room, please."

I shuffled out and down the stairs. I pulled out my phone and called Dawn.

"Pray," I said as soon as she answered. "I don't know if I am going to have a job anymore in about ten minutes."

"What?" she cried.

"The board is voting on whether or not they need to fire me and put a new executive director in my place. Someone with a better record of fundraising, I guess."

Unlike David, I have never had anyone—I don't think—who wanted to kill me, at least not anyone I would consider a friend. However, there have been a couple times I've had to weather a storm or two that arose from internal sources.

As Chestnut Mountain Ranch started to pick up momentum, there was a small movement within the board of directors questioning whether or not I was the man to lead the ministry to the next level. We had high aspirations, and it was certainly true that I did not have much experience with growing large nonprofits. This was my first attempt.

I don't want to point any fingers, and I certainly believe that it is OK to raise questions about your leadership. I don't expect to be immune from evaluation. If I am not the best guy for the job, then so be it. Vote me out. No hard feelings.

The point I am trying to make is I've had to persevere through some doubts and opposition, even on my own team. People have questioned me, pushed back, and resisted my leadership. I could have folded to that pressure or stood up and faced it. But I decided to hang on and see how things would turn out. And like David, I trusted that God would sustain me through it all.

David never lashed out at Absalom, he never criticized him, and when his son died he wept at the loss. And through it all David trusted God, and God delivered him and his throne in the end.

Those 15 minutes or so the board took to vote were some of the longest, most stressful of my life. I was sure God had called me to lead this ministry, but my calling was all hanging in the balance at that moment. Fortunately, they decided that I was, in fact, the one who should be leading Chestnut Mountain Ranch, and I kept my job.

It would have been easy to lose confidence at that point, to question my calling, to just throw in the towel, but it was through that experience that, remarkably, God cemented even more in my own mind the vision He called me to. Sometimes it takes a little opposition and struggle to really understand and to be the kind of leaders God wants us to be.

Most of the New Testament seems to be written with the underlying tone and (maybe not-so-subtle) admonishment to persevere. Paul wrote to the Thessalonians to "hold fast" (2 Thessalonians 2:15). He wrote to the Ephesian and Corinthian churches to "stand firm" (Ephesians 6:14; 1 Corinthians 16:13). Peter wrote to the Christians scattered throughout Pontus, Galatia, Cappadocia, Asia, and Bithynia to stand firm (1 Peter 5:9). And the writer of Hebrews encouraged his readers to hold on (Hebrews 10:23).

All this underscores that perseverance is a central part of what we are to be doing as Christians and followers of God. God calls us to persevere through opposition and conflict, when the bombshells are falling all around and we can hardly take a breath, but many times the most difficult season to hold fast in is when there is silence. It is one thing to keep our resolve when there's lots of action. It is quite another when it seems like nothing is happening.

We live in a college town in West Virginia. Many people move here for school or work, so it is a pretty active and lively place. And active, vibrant communities tend to, for some reason, attract a lot of church planters. I can see why. Most people want to plant churches where things are happening, where there are young people and families open to new ideas and new ways of doing things.

Our town certainly fits that bill.

I am not sure what would count as a "normal" amount of church plants in a given city, but we seem to have more than our share. I think in the last year I heard of at least four that were getting started. That may have been an abnormally high year, but I'd say we average a couple per year. In a town of more than 100,000 residents, including students, that is a lot of churches being started.

Now, don't get me wrong. I am all for church planting and planters. We have scores of people not going to church anywhere, so my hope is that all these planters are connecting with people and introducing them to Jesus. We need lots of gospel-preaching churches.

Unfortunately, I see a lot of churches being planted with much fanfare and gusto, and then most if not all of those churches close down after a year or two. They seem to run out of steam. I don't know the reasons behind most of the closings, but I do know one thing: it has to do with perseverance.

One of the churches I attended when I first came to West Virginia is one of the largest in the state, but it wasn't that way at the beginning. Started in the mid-80s, the church met in a daycare center for close to a decade, with only a few dozen families and a handful of students. There was virtually no growth for well over ten years.

It is easy to get discouraged in that kind of situation because you wonder if God is still behind what you're doing. Ten years is plenty of time to start wondering what is going on and why it seems like God is not showing up. But I've learned God is usually not in as much of a hurry as we are. Joseph spent years as a slave and prisoner in Egypt. Moses waited 40 years as a shepherd. Israel was 400 years under the thumb of various pharaohs. David waited years for his throne. And the Messiah took a really long time to show up.

In the meantime, silence. God didn't say a whole lot. And silence will test anyone's resolve.

After about ten years, the church started to really grow. They went from about 150 to 900 in four years and then to close to 3,000 in the next five. They have a huge influence in our town. Imagine if they had not persevered through those silent years. What if they had quit, packed up, and went home? They would have missed out on some pretty great things.

I have sat down with a fair number of these new church planters over the years. They invite me to speak at their churches, and sometimes I can see the strain of silence, the weight of waiting on their faces. I can hear it in their voices.

My encouragement to them is to hold on, stand firm to what you have been called to by God. God is not in a huge hurry. He is going to get done what He wants to get done, and our job is to just trust that He knows what He is doing and to persevere even when we don't hear from Him for a while.

In the cases of a few failed church plants, I thought that if they had just held on a little longer, they could have become thriving churches. I think they just quit a little too soon, maybe because they didn't perceive enough to be happening.

There are a few good examples in the Bible of men and women who persevered even when God was silent. One of the most impressive in my mind is Job.

He is amazing, if you ask me, because not only was he not seeing growth but also he was experiencing extreme regression: all his kids died, and he lost all of his livestock, servants, and crops. And he was stricken with boils and ailments. And God was silent through it all. Didn't say a word. Job didn't get it, he didn't like it, but that was what was going on. His friends gave what I think was probably sound advice, given the circumstances, and all that he had endured: curse God and die.

But Job never gave up; he never lost faith. He suffered greatly, but he persevered to the end. And he was pretty adamant about it, declaring to his friends, "Though he slay me, yet will I hope in him" (Job 13:15). That's perseverance, to death. And after death, it's over, and that's when we get to rest.

I wonder how many pastors and other leaders have Job's kind of fortitude—when everything was going in the very wrong direction, they still continue to trust and hope and wait on God. That's a real challenge but one that we should all be prepared to face because there is going to come a time when each of us is going to have to hold on and endure a season of silence, a time when not much is going on. And if you aren't ready for it, you could get derailed, and you might just quit. And, who knows? You may quit right before God is ready to do something incredible.

That first year when we were at the end of our cash supply and had gained little traction, I often wondered what we were doing. We only had 88 contacts on our mailing list and still had been unable to find land to purchase.

Maybe I am just stubborn—that helps for sure—but I was also convicted God had called us and would show up when we really needed Him. Daniel persevered through nearly a month of prayer and fasting before a messenger from God showed up. I don't know if you have ever fasted for a month, but that will be the longest month of your life, I guarantee.

I admit at the end of that first year, I told Dawn that if we didn't see something happen soon, we might have to move back to Atlanta. I didn't want to go, but I sensed we were running out of time. And if God didn't show up soon we might have to call it quits.

I am glad we didn't give up because by the end of that year our little group of contacts had raised more than $700K, and we had 224 acres for Chestnut Mountain Ranch. Let me encourage you to persevere and remember in the darkness what God revealed to you in the light.

TOOL NO. 7:
WISDOM

Once upon a time there was a young man who was told by a very powerful king that he could have anything he wanted. He could have riches, power, anything at all. If he were one of several kids I know who are about his age, he would have asked for a new gaming system or smartphone.

But this kid was different: he asked for wisdom. Seems like he already had it, to be honest.

You may have guessed I was describing Solomon, and he had just ascended to the throne after the death of his father, the king of Israel, David. Soon after he assumed the throne, God comes and makes an offer that is stunning:

> At Gibeon the LORD appeared to Solomon during the night in a dream, and God said, "Ask for whatever you want me to give you." Solomon answered, "You have shown great kindness to your servant, my father David, because he was faithful to you and righteous and upright in heart. You have continued this great kindness to him and have given him a son to sit on this throne this very day. Now, LORD my God, you have made your servant king in place of my father David. But I am only a little child and do not know how to carry out my duties. Your servant is here among the people you have chosen, a great people, too numerous to count or number. So give your servant a discerning heart to govern your people and to distinguish between right and wrong. For who is able to govern this great people of yours?"
>
> —1 Kings 3:5–8

God was obviously pleased because He not only promised to make Solomon the wisest man on the planet, but He also gave him astounding wealth and a reputation beyond any person on the planet. "Moreover, I will give you what you have not asked for—

both wealth and honor—so that in your lifetime you will have no equal among kings" (1 Kings 3:13).

Yeah, that's better than a gaming system.

What strikes me is not so much that Solomon asked for wisdom, although that was brilliant, but why he asked for it. He understood something about himself: he knew he was only a child and did not know how to be king.

Maybe that was a foregone conclusion in his own mind; he had been on the throne for a short time when God came to him, and he already had a fair amount of drama: He had to execute his brother and a couple of others for treason. His mother was a real pain too. Under those circumstances I am guessing he figured out pretty quickly he had no idea what he was doing.

Anyone who seeks to follow God's leading is going to come to the realization at some point that that they, like Solomon, are struggling to figure out the right course of action. We will be faced with difficult decisions and unknown roads. The only question is: will we have the humility to ask for help? Solomon knew and was willing to admit he was only a kid, and when he had the opportunity, he asked God for wisdom. It was the best choice he could have made.

Before Dawn and I moved to West Virginia, we spent a few years at Eagle Ranch near Atlanta. We were thrown in the deep end, so to speak, and we figured out quickly we had very little idea what we were doing as houseparents. One thing we discovered when you are thrown in a pool and realize you can't swim, you cannot be too proud to ask for some help getting out.

Wisdom works like that. It comes to those who are humble enough to ask and look for it. It is no coincidence that Solomon began his book of wisdom, Proverbs, with the declaration: "The fear of the LORD is the beginning of knowledge" (Proverbs 1:7). What he means is that if you want wisdom—and trust me you do—then it starts with humility and a respect for those smarter than you, especially God.

We are so thankful we had a number of folks at Eagle Ranch to lean on. There were many days we were pushed to our limits and felt like we were drowning, and we were not shy in asking for advice and direction when we needed it. We had no room for pride.

Humility is the first step toward wisdom. Those who see themselves like Solomon, given an awesome responsibility to lead the people of God but also young and inexperienced and certainly not having all the answers, are the ones who will find wisdom and ultimately success.

"Hey, Steve, you want to go walk that property with me?"

I looked up from my notebook, scribbling a last few thoughts from the recently ended staff meeting, to see Eddie Staub standing in the door about to step out. I was a bit caught off guard and looked at him with what must have been a completely blank stare.

"You know, the 300 acres we were just talking about. The land we are thinking about buying."

"Oh yeah," I nodded clearing my head and catching up with his train of thought. "Yeah, sure, that'd be great."

Eddie Staub is the founder of Eagle Ranch. An ex-college baseball player from Alabama, Eddie started his home for children from nothing and raised up a program that is nationally known as one of the best children's homes in the country. I didn't know anyone who understood how to do it better. That was a bit intimidating; I didn't want him to think I was a total goof, but I also had enough smarts to know that I needed his help if I was going to get my dream of a ranch in West Virginia started.

This little impromptu hike would be the perfect chance to pitch my idea and ask for some advice. I knew I didn't know what I was doing. I was a little worried he would see through that, but I decided I had to swallow my pride and just get it out there.

"Dawn and I are thinking about starting a home in West Virginia," I said after we had been walking for about five minutes. I remember distinctly how loud the sticks seemed to be breaking under our steps. It was the most silent the world had ever been.

> HUMILITY IS THE NUMBER-ONE KEY TO WISDOM, TO FINDING THE RIGHT PATH GOD HAS FOR US.

"I am going to need your help and advice along the way," I continued.

We must have talked for three hours that afternoon and lots more over the coming months as we prepared for our move. Eddie's advice was invaluable. We never could have made it without the help and wisdom he and many others at Eagle Ranch shared with us.

Humility is the number-one key to wisdom, to finding the right path God has for us. If we can approach God and others as children do, with some deference and respect, we may walk away with more than we could have imagined. Like when Solomon got a lot more than he hoped for, all for a little humility and asking for wisdom.

I love James's encouragement at the beginning of his letter: "But if any of you lacks wisdom, let him ask of God, who gives to all generously and without reproach, and it will be given to him" (James 1:5 NASB).

That's a pretty good offer, if you ask me.

"We can't stay here forever."

I looked at my partner Danny, who was sitting in the passenger seat of the 1983 GMC truck we were staked out in, over the collar of my coat. He was right, of course. I looked up through the window of the truck at the streetlight overhead. We could hear the constant hum of electricity. Outside there was an occasional shout or yell. Someone laughed loudly and others joined in. The street was abuzz with activity.

I shifted my weight, I could feel the edge of the seat buckle digging into my side. My right knee was jammed against the steering column and starting to ache. My back and neck were stiff.

"Yeah," I replied, shifting again hoping for a more comfortable position. "We're not going to see anything from here."

I looked at my watch. 11:30 p.m.

Danny and I were investigating a murder suspect in an especially rough section of Atlanta. We knew our target had gang ties, and so we needed to operate undercover and with extreme caution. We followed several leads, and the most recent led us out that night. We were parked outside the suspect's mother's home and were hoping to get a look in the backyard to see if his car was there. We had been looking for him for nearly three months.

Two men sitting in a truck for hours would undoubtedly raise a few eyebrows, which is why we had spent the last two hours hunched down, out of sight. But we couldn't sit there forever, and the streets were getting a little more crowded. Eventually someone would see us. We had to make a move.

"Let's go for a walk," I said to Danny. "Stay in the shadows as much as you can. We'll just take a peek in the backyard and then head out."

As we stepped into the street, I could feel my heart racing. This was a notorious gang neighborhood and well-known for frequent violent activity. I pulled my collar up a little higher to try not to stand out. I am not sure it worked, but we went unnoticed by the half dozen or so people sitting on front porches and on the sidewalks. We stepped quickly into the street and crossed. We had parked about two houses from our target, and within 20 seconds we found ourselves in the narrow walkway between his house and a neighbor's. Both homes were dark. A street lamp in the back alley cast a triangular wedge of light onto the ground. We pushed ourselves into the dark against the house and slowly crept, hoping to catch a glimpse of something helpful.

To be honest, it felt a little like a movie. We had no idea what was in that backyard, so we crept as silently as we could. The house appeared empty. All the lights were off, and we could hear no talking. Somewhere in the distance, we could hear a police siren come on and then disappear into the distance.

My senses were in overdrive. I felt every crack and ridge in the uneven concrete. My eyes adjusted and were finely tuned to the darkness. Even though there was no moon, I could see everything with daylight clarity. Every step echoed in my ears, and I winced when I kicked a small rocked and it skidded across the ground. It sounded like a boulder bouncing down a hill. I could smell someone barbecuing burgers, maybe two streets over.

Danny was the first down the walkway, his silhouette pressed against the house as he edged ever so carefully along the wall. One step then another, we slowly approached the corner of the house. Another three steps and we would be able to see into the backyard. Every step or two, I glanced over my shoulder to check our rear. It was empty. All the talking and movement in the front street seemed to have stopped as well.

Danny took another step and then a second. One step and we'd be there. I felt my throat tighten, and I took a slow deep breath. I tried to swallow, but my mouth was dry and my throat tight.

One more step. Danny leaned toward the edge of the building then started to walk around the corner.

There are moments when you don't think, you just react, not for any empirical or logical reason but simply out of instinct. As soon as Danny started to take that last step out of the alley and into the backyard, my hand involuntarily shot out and grabbed him by the arm. He stopped immediately and froze. There was no reason to stop him, other than I had a feeling we needed to wait just a few seconds more in the alley.

He looked back at me, and I signaled to stay quiet. We both looked into the backyard. The street lamp was bright, and as we looked up, we saw a small cloud of blue smoke emerge from around the corner. We recognized the smell immediately—cigarette smoke. Someone was right there—a guard or sentry perhaps—and we had almost walked right into him.

Our hearts were racing. We backed even more slowly down the alley. And when we got back to the truck we looked at each other but didn't say a word the whole way back to the station.

I believe the Holy Spirit caused me to reach out and stop my partner, which may have prevented us from stepping into a full-on gun battle that night. I don't know how else to explain what happened when I grabbed Danny. I just had a sense, in an instant, that we needed to stop and wait. And that turned out, incredibly, to be a very wise decision.

When Jesus was getting ready to go to the Cross and to leave His disciples, He told them that although He would be gone, He would send the Holy Spirit whose primary job would be to guide those belonging to Jesus. The Apostle John recorded what Jesus said in his Gospel: "But when he, the Spirit of truth, comes, he will guide you into all truth" (John 16:13).

That's a pretty good inside track to wisdom. And I think the Spirit of God guided us that night and many nights since we started Chestnut Mountain Ranch.

Anyone who is going to follow the call of God is going to have to learn to listen to the Holy Spirit because the Holy Spirit will always guide us in a way that is true, good, and profitable. I believe that true wisdom comes from developing an acute ear, able to listen to the Holy Spirit.

Consider the story of Philip in the New Testament. He was just minding his own business when an angel showed up and told him he needed to go on a little walk into the desert and get himself to the road that lead from Jerusalem to Gaza.

I wish the Spirit was as overt with me—maybe He is and I am just not a very good listener. In any case, Philip hops right up and goes, and while he is walking along he meets the chariot of an important Ethiopian eunuch, an official in charge of all the queen's money.

The Spirit tells Philip to "go to that chariot and stay near it" (Acts 8:29). Directions don't get much more simple or obvious than that, but still if I were in Philip's shoes, I may have at least asked what in the world was going on. But Philip simply obeys and runs alongside the guy, which was probably a pretty comical scene in and of itself. The Ethiopian is reading the Book of Isaiah, and Philip sees an opening to tell him about Jesus, the man in the passage Isaiah is referring to. The Ethiopian believes, gets baptized, and Philip assumes the world record for the easiest and quickest conversion in history.

And then it gets really cool. The Holy Spirit reenters and seems to zap Philip like he is in a *Star Trek* movie to another town, several miles away:

> *When they came up out of the water, the Spirit of the Lord suddenly took Philip away, and the eunuch did not see him again, but went on his way rejoicing. Philip, however, appeared at Azotus and traveled about, preaching the gospel in all the towns until he reached Caesarea.*
> *—Acts 8:39–40*

This story has been an encouragement for me to do my best to consult and listen to the Holy Spirit. When He is involved and guiding me, two things are going to happen: I am going to be pretty effective and make good decisions, and things are going to be exciting, even miraculous.

I don't get it entirely. I don't get exactly how the Holy Spirit reveals things to us like this. I don't know how I knew to pull Danny back from that corner, but I did. And it might have saved our lives. Hearing from God in that way is a bit miraculous and crazy, but it happens. And I think the better we know God and trust Him and practice listening to the Holy Spirit, the better decisions and wiser we will be.

When I was a kid—like many of my friends and other children who grew up in my generation—my favorite television show was *CHiPs*, the exciting fast-paced show about two cops riding motorcycles and chasing down the bad guys as part of the California Highway Patrol. I would lay awake at night and think about joining Jon Baker and Frank "Ponch" Poncherello in taking down the bad guys of southern California.

A few years later, it was Crockett and Tubbs racing around the waters of Miami that caught my attention and imagination. *Miami Vice.* How awesome would that be? Fast boats, cool linen suits and pastel-colored shirts, and apparently shaving was optional. Sign me up.

When you are young and lacking experience, you tend to believe everything that happens on television is exactly how it happens in real life: the cars, gun fights, fancy clothes, and beautiful houses. When you grow up, you realize life is actually not like that at all.

As I entered college, I was still captivated by the allure of what I thought was the glamour of law enforcement life. I decided to major in criminal justice with the thought they would probably just straight issue me a Ferrari and white linen sport coat upon graduation.

My senior year we had to write a paper based upon an interview with a real police officer or someone in the business. Somehow I landed a meeting with the director of the Drug Enforcement Agency, the DEA, at their Atlanta offices.

I was more than a little intimidated walking into the building. I was stopped at the front door and asked my business. I told them the person I was there to meet and was directed to proceed through a door at the end of the lobby.

The hallway I entered was like none I had ever been in before. No doors, just a long passage way that seemed to go nowhere. It must have been a quarter of a mile long. Not a single window, air vent, drain, or other opening to be seen. Just the hum of fluorescent lights echoing off the blank white walls. The air was sterile, like the inside of a swimming pool that had been emptied of water. Eventually I came upon a single white door. I tried to open it, but it was locked. A second later, I heard a buzz and then a click, so I tried again. This time it opened.

The room I stepped into was about as opposite the hallway as one could get. I am guessing there were a couple hundred cubicles and twice as many people working, talking, and bustling about. The sound of conversations and keyboards, shuffling papers, and ringing phones made the room electric.

It was pretty cool, and I was excited at the thought that I might get to be part of this kind of life. I was a bit concerned that I didn't see any sunglasses-wearing, wise-cracking detectives working the room, causing all kinds of laughter and mayhem, which everyone ignored because these trouble-making agents had just brought down a whole cartel over breakfast. But I figured that maybe they had just left to work on their tans and facial scruff. Suffice it to say, I had a vivid imagination.

A young man, maybe in his midtwenties approached and asked if I was there to see the director. I said I was, and he indicated I should follow him. We made our way past dozens of hardworking agents, and after knocking on an office door in the back corner of the room and hearing a gruff, "Come in!" he opened the door, turned to me and smiled, and left me to enter on my own.

To my surprise, the director smiled as I walked in, and he asked me to sit down.

"So you have an interest in law enforcement?" he asked.

"Yes, sir, I do, ever since I was a little kid." I could feel a small pool of sweat starting to collect in the small of my back.

"Well, it is an exciting life and an invigorating job," he continued. "You'll never experience anything like it. But there are some huge tradeoffs."

I nodded as if I already knew everything he was going to say, which I most assuredly did not.

"Here, take a look at this." He grabbed a packet of papers from his desk and threw them down in front of me. At the top, in bold letters were the words *Application, Drug Enforcement Agency.* Beneath was a paragraph with the header *Before You Begin.*

That caught my attention.

I went on to read and soon discovered some hard truths about the life I had dreamt about since I was just a kid. The gist of the paragraph was this: The life of a DEA agent, while exciting, is not for everyone. If accepted as an agent, I would be expected to move often, maybe several times a year to various locations around the country and even overseas. There could be times when I would not be able to talk to family or friends, months at a time. The current divorce rate for DEA agents was 86 percent.

I looked up from the page.

"It's not for everyone," he said, understanding what I was thinking.

I never filled out that application. In fact, I still have it because it reminds me of the challenges we may not see or anticipate in life. And I am so thankful I was able to talk to someone who knew a little more than me and for the absolute wisdom he was able to impart.

Wisdom comes from seeking good counsel. And a wise person knows enough to know that they don't know it all and will seek out others to help them find the best path forward. I have always loved Proverbs 15:22 and tried to apply it as often as I can: "Plans fail for lack of counsel, but with many advisers they succeed."

When we are young, we think we know it all and typically tend to refuse the advice and counsel of others. We don't consult our parents or friends or others who may have more experience. We just dive in and assume we are smart enough to figure it out. Some of us are fortunate enough to have people who love us and show us the error in that kind of thinking. The best leaders, the smartest people, all have people they trust and who have spoken up to show them a better way.

A great example of this type of person is Moses. Possibly the greatest leader in the history of Israel, he was tapped by God to shepherd a few million people out of slavery and from under the heavy hand of the mightiest empire on the planet at the time, Egypt. And with the obvious help from God, he did it, basically single-handedly. He took them through the Red Sea and out in the desert, picking up the Ten Commandments on the way. It's pretty impressive if you think about it.

Not long after they escaped captivity, Moses met up with his father-in-law, with whom he had lived and worked for 40 years prior to his calling to emancipate God's people. Moses, I imagine, was pretty excited to tell his wife's father all that had happened. My understanding is most sons-in-law have an instinctual need to impress their in-laws. I am guessing Moses was no different.

In Exodus 18, we read that the next day Moses took his seat to listen and judge various disputes among the people. As you can imagine, with a group numbering in the millions, that was going to take some time. Moses sat and listened to people from morning until evening.

Jethro observed what was going on and asked Moses about it. Moses explained that he was the one who settled the disputes, and that's how peace was kept in the camp. Jethro's response is pretty funny:

> *What you are doing is not good. You and these people who come to you will only wear yourselves out. The work is too heavy for for you; you cannot handle it alone. Listen to me now and I will give you some advice, and may God be with you.*
>
> *—Exodus 18:17–19*

Jethro suggested appointing officials over thousands, hundreds, fifties, and tens. They would handle the lesser disputes, and only the most difficult cases would be brought to Moses to weigh in on.

It was a brilliant idea, one that maybe Moses would have thought of himself—but he didn't. And what's more, he didn't get offended or threatened or dismissive. Instead, he listened to wise counsel: "Moses listened to his father-in-law and did everything he said" (v. 24). And I bet his life was a lot better off for that little bit of wisdom he got from Jethro.

ANYONE WHO IS FOLLOWING GOD'S CALL WOULD DO WELL TO SEEK THE ADVICE AND COUNSEL OF OTHERS WHO HAVE GONE BEFORE.

Anyone who is following God's call would do well to seek the advice and counsel of others who have gone before. Eddie Staub and others at Eagle Ranch have been a huge and wonderful resource. In fact, they began an initiative to help guys like me wanting to start homes. Their approach was to scare away as many people as possible, kind of like the DEA, but hey, I am stubborn! And there are many others along the way who have helped guide me and on whose wisdom I have relied. To all of them I am eternally grateful.

Anyone who has ever tried to do something new and follow God's calling should immediately recognize the value and importance of wisdom. If you make foolish decisions, you will not be in business for very long. We have discussed in this chapter three ways that we get wisdom: by being humble enough to ask, by being sensitive to the Holy Spirit's leading, and by seeking the counsel of others who have gone before. But I think there is at least one more important step to attaining wisdom: obedience. Jesus says, in the Gospel of Matthew:

> *Therefore everyone who hears these words of mine and puts them into practice is like a wise man who built his house on the rock. The rain came down, the streams rose, and the winds blew and beat against that house; yet it did not fall, because it had its foundation on the rock.*
>
> —*Matthew 7:24–25*

Jesus is making an explicit connection between wisdom and the act of putting that wisdom into practice. In other words, obedience. Wisdom is pretty much useless if it is not applied. You can get all the advice in the world, but if you don't use it then it makes no difference.

I was reading the Gospel of Mark the other day and came across the section where Jesus describes the farmer who is sowing the seeds of the Word into various soils. Some receive it and grow and are fruitful, but most end up being unfruitful for various reasons: trouble, worries, Satan. Right after Jesus talks about a lamp and how it is meant to be set on a lampstand, not hidden. He warns His listeners to pay attention to what He is saying. Then He adds:

> *"Consider carefully what you hear," he continued. "With the measure you use, it will be measured to you—and even more. Whoever has will be given more; whoever does not have, even what they have will be taken from them."*
>
> *—Mark 4:24–25*

This whole section is about receiving the word, light, knowledge, and wisdom from God. Jesus tells His followers that if you do not use the wisdom and insight God gives, then you will eventually lose it. And if you do use it, even more will come your way.

I think this is kind of what Jesus had in mind when He said:

> *Do not give dogs what is sacred; do not throw your pearls to pigs. If you do, they may trample them under their feet, and turn and tear you to pieces.*
>
> *—Matthew 7:6*

God does not give valuable things, like wisdom, to people who cannot appreciate it, or who He knows won't follow it.

There are a lot of reasons why obeying good advice may be difficult: it could require a lot of effort, time, inconvenience, or money. But the risk is that God, the Holy Spirit, and others are going to stop giving you good advice if you never take it, if you never act on it.

TOOL NO. 8:
PERSPECTIVE

I t is hard for me to believe that after ten years and countless hours in meetings and prayer and hundreds of thousands of miles sharing the story of what God is doing to anyone who would listen, Chestnut Mountain Ranch is up and running. We have boys who are being loved and challenged. We have one home finished and another under construction. And while, in many ways, we are just getting started, it feels sometimes like God has brought us a really long way.

PERSPECTIVE IS THE ABILITY TO SEE YOURSELF, YOUR WORK, AND THOSE AROUND YOU AS GOD SEES THEM.

One of the most important tools for any leader, yet one of the least discussed, is perspective. Most leaders I know are so engaged, so passionate about what they have been called to do, it can be very difficult to separate themselves from the work and see how it fits into what God cares about on a more global level.

In fact, I would go so far as to say that perspective is the ability to see yourself, your work, and those around you as God sees them. He has and is the ultimate vantage point, and we should always try to see things as He does. This takes work and diligence, and we will never fully be able to do it. But I think there are at least three reasons perspective is important for a leader: it protects our identity, shapes our methodology, and increases our motivation. Without perspective we may lose our true self, we may compromise our values and mission, and we may lose heart and quit.

"Steve, I've been coaching football for more than four decades, and that is just the nature of the beast."

I looked across the table. His eyes were narrow and focused. His skin—wrinkled, leathery and familiar like a well-used sofa or coat—reflected a career spent in the sun, wind, and rain. He was a man who had weathered the elements and, I could tell, enjoyed every minute of it.

"You are going to have seasons when you win more than you lose," he continued. "And you are going to have seasons when you lose more than you win. God knows, I've had plenty of both."

I smiled. I had grown up watching Coach Nehlen's teams play. I adored the West Virginia Mountaineers and, like almost every other kid in the state, dreamed of one day playing for the gold-and-blue. I remember the joy that swept through our house on those wonderful fall Saturday afternoons when our team was winning. I can still hear the whoops and cheers and the cars honking as the final musket exploded, signaling another victory for the Mountaineers.

Coach Don Nehlen is a hero to many. People joke he should run for governor. We all figured he could do that in his spare time during the week. Saturdays, he'd be busy leading our team to another win.

But then, I also remember the losses, the missed opportunities, the streak of bowl game defeats, the losing seasons. It was hard to go to school on the weeks our team lost; a dour cloud of despair and anxiety would hang over our classrooms and all over town. Every head hung lower those days leading up to the next game, when we hoped the outcome would be better.

And when one loss turned into another and another, we all knew this season was lost, and there would be no bowl game, no bragging rights, no mention on the nightly sports shows of the Mountaineers as one of the country's elite. It was then people would started talking about maybe it was time for Coach to hang it up—his methods were outdated, he was getting outcoached and outrecruited. The game had passed him by. Maybe we should start to look around for some-one else.

I looked at coach. He smiled knowingly.

"I have been doing this for 40 years," he repeated, "and one thing I have learned is that you have to find a way to remove yourself from any one individual season, to not let that define who you are. There are going to be highs and lows, wins and losses, but that cannot define you. Your foundation, your identity has to be rooted in something else."

I nodded because I knew he was right. It was easy to get caught up in the highs of ministry. It was equally tempting to be pulled low by the challenges and setbacks. What I needed was a perspective from which to observe and evaluate and understand what was happening with Chestnut Mountain Ranch that didn't, at the same time, throw my identity around like a rag doll.

"We used to have these cookouts every week with my coaching staff," Coach looked over my shoulder and into the distance, remembering. "All our families would be there: wives, kids, everyone. Usually on Sunday night. We would laugh and joke and carry on and all eat together.

"That was our foundation: our friendship, our trust and loyalty to one another. It didn't matter what happened that weekend in the game; we knew we all cared about one another and that the opinions of a whole state of fans, good or bad, couldn't touch us there. Those nights gave us perspective; it was just a game—and we did our best and worked our tails off to win—but at the end of the day we had people who loved us no matter what. And that enabled us to ignore all the noise from the outside, all the rain against the shutters."

YOU AND WHAT YOU DO ARE TWO DIFFERENT THINGS.

If you are a leader, you are going to go through both fruitful and lean years. Like coach said, it is just the nature of the beast. The problem comes when we are unable to extract our identity, who we are and how we view ourselves, from those wins and losses.

If, for you, the highs are too high and the lows are too low, then it is likely that you need to step back, separate yourself—who you are—from what you do. You need to gain some perspective: you and what you do are two different things.

Aside from Jesus, there is probably not a person in the Bible who experienced more of the ups and downs of leadership than David. He was a tremendous warrior and led Israel to its pinnacle as a political force. No nation was able to stand against his armies. And yet he suffered humiliation at home; his own son and his best friend's father tried to have him killed. And while his psalms are filled with copious praise and happiness as well as gut-wrenching pain and sorrow, they—almost without fail—cry out to God for protection, for provision, for shelter. Time and again, David calls God his "Rock," his foundation. The place from which he can find respite from the ups and downs of life.

That's a pretty good perspective.

Several years ago one of my friends went through a divorce. He told me that as devastating as it was, God used that situation to solidify something about his identity. He said he had a choice: either listen to the voice of rejection coming from his wife, about how he was a bad husband and she didn't love him any more, or listen to what God had to say about him.

WE NEED TO GET GOD'S PERSPECTIVE ON WHO WE ARE BECAUSE IF WE DO NOT, THEN THE VOICES, THE PRAISE AND THE CRITICISM, WILL START TO AFFECT AND DISRUPT AND ULTIMATELY DISTORT OUR IDENTITY.

We need to get God's perspective on who we are because if we do not, then the voices, the praise and the criticism, will start to affect and disrupt and ultimately distort our identity.

My friend said he spent a lot of time right after his wife left in the Book of Ephesians, especially the first chapter. "I go back to those verses often," he would tell me. "They remind me that I am loved, chosen, forgiven, and secure because of Jesus. My circumstances may shift and fluctuate, but how God sees me stays constant and that keeps me steady and able to move forward in a positive way."

While it is important to sees ourselves from God's perspective when we are enduring criticism and defeat, it may be even more vital to stay close to Him during times of success and praise. As the director of Chestnut Mountain Ranch, I tend to get a lot of the accolades thrown my way for the good things happening. I am not going to lie, it is nice to have people say good things about what you are doing and accomplishing.

But it is really easy to get a distorted view of yourself too. Remember Nebuchadnezzar? There is a similar story about Herod recorded in the Book of Acts. He gave a speech, and people loved it; they said his was the voice of God not man. He didn't correct them, so God struck him dead and worms ate his body.

He probably could have benefited from a better perspective on who he really was. He was a leader, no doubt, but only because God put him there. And God could, and did, take him out just as easily.

I, for one, would prefer to keep an honest, accurate view of myself—God's view, His perspective—and I really don't want to be eaten by worms. I doubt you do either.

"Hey, Johnny, you want to come out of there for a second?" I leaned against the door frame and peered into the small but tidy room. In one corner was a single bed, neatly made. Opposite and next to the door was a chest of drawers. The surface was clear except for a pen and notebook. A lamp stood on a small table next to the bed. A picture of a mountain landscape on the far wall opposite the door was the only decoration. A closed closet door was the only other item of note in the room.

It was to the door I was speaking.

"Hey, I really want to talk to you, do you think you could give me just five minutes?"

Johnny was relatively new to our home at Eagle Ranch. By all accounts he wasn't a bad kid. He had done fairly well in school, had a few friends, but slowly, over time, had become more and more distant and reclusive and had withdrawn and refused to speak to anyone. Eventually he landed with us. His parents did not know what else to do.

And I wasn't having much luck either. Johnny had been hiding in the closet for more than four hours.

"OK, well there's dinner on the kitchen counter when you get hungry. We saved you a plate. Fried chicken. I think you'll like it."

Johnny was just one kid out the dozens at Eagle Ranch at that time. Just one kid. I had six others who needed my attention too. Sometimes it was draining the amount of effort this one boy took with little to no response or reciprocation.

I stuck my head back in the door. "Oh, and I love you. Just so you know." I heard him shift in the closet, and I knew he heard me. I smiled and closed the door.

When I first arrived at Eagle Ranch, they told me my job was to lead these young men, to help them become godly and upright, and to teach them to one day lead their own families. Sometimes, I confess, it was frustrating because, while I was ready to lead, they did not seem ready to follow.

Maybe you have experienced this in your attempts to lead.

I wanted to be a great leader, but it was pretty obvious I needed a change of perspective to have a better grasp of what God thought.

> *Jesus called [the disciples] together and said, "You know that those who are regarded as rulers of the Gentiles lord it over them, and their high officials exercise authority over them. Not so with you. Instead, whoever wants to become great among you must be your servant, and whoever wants to be first must be slave of all. For even the Son of Man did not come to be served, but to serve, and to give his life as a ransom for many."*
> *—Mark 10:42–45*

This is probably as shocking a perspective today as it was back then. Jesus is telling his disciples that if anyone wants to be great, it is not about how many people fall under your authority or how many minions you get to boss around. That's not what makes you a great leader. What makes you a great leader is how well you serve others. God's perspective is that the great ones serve, they don't demand service. They want to see others succeed and become all they can for God.

If you are getting into ministry because you want someone to follow you, then you have the wrong idea of things. If you are instead interested in launching others, encouraging them, resourcing them, helping them to go beyond and leave you watching them in the distance, then you probably are on the right track.

I am amazed at John the Baptist's perspective about Jesus; he himself was a pretty popular dude. Huge crowds were following *him*, until Jesus showed up. Then his own followers started deserting him and taking up with the new guy. The crazy thing is that John encouraged it. When asked about this by his own disciples, John simply replied, "He must become greater; I must become less" (John 3:30).

John had the view that he was there to introduce and, in some sense, launch Jesus' career and ministry. He understood that was his unique role. It was never about him, and for this reason, Jesus said there was no one greater than John.

It took some time for me to get through to Johnny. I spent hours talking to him, encouraging him, loving him. I kept at it, day after day, even though there were other kids making more progress, others more willing to get behind me and follow. It would have been easy to just let him go. After all, what did I have to gain from one kid?

But something in me really wanted to see Johnny become what I knew he could become. And to reach him, I was willing to sacrifice other pursuits that may have benefited me. It was a long road, but slowly he started to respond and emerge from his shell. By the time Dawn and I left Eagle Ranch, he was a completely different kid. I wish I could take credit, but God had gotten hold of his heart. Johnny was no longer the recluse I met when he first arrived.

WHEN YOU BECOME A LEADER, YOU CAN HOLD TO THE IDEA THAT LEADERSHIP IS ABOUT YOUR NAME, YOUR REPUTATION, AND YOUR BAND OF FOLLOWERS. OR IT CAN BE ABOUT LAUNCHING OTHERS, SEEING THEM SUCCEED WHILE YOU CHEER THEM ON FROM BEHIND THE SCENES.

One day, after we had moved to West Virginia I got a letter from Johnny. He was writing to tell us that he was feeling God call him into full-time ministry and that he was going to spend a year abroad as a missionary. He was writing to ask us for some financial support. I have never been so happy to write a check in my whole life.

Johnny helped me realize something. When you become a leader, you can hold to the idea that leadership is about your name, your reputation, and your band of followers. Or it can be about launching others, seeing them succeed while you cheer them on from behind the scenes. It makes a profound difference which approach you choose. And ultimately, it matters greatly to God as well.

Our administration building at Chestnut Mountain Ranch is located on a pretty steep hill in the middle of our property, and from where I sit in my office, I can look out down the narrow valley over thousands of beautiful hardwood trees. In the summer, the sun and deep greens of the forest, the gentle breezes that run up the dirt road to us, are almost hypnotic. In the fall, the explosion of reds and oranges and yellows cause my pulse to quicken.

I like the view because it gets me up above the trees, and sometimes I feel like that is where I need to be—up out of the day-to-day noise and activity, up where it is clear—and I can hopefully gain some perspective.

In between our building on the hill and the road is a small retaining pond. It is not very big, maybe the size of an average swimming pool and not as deep. Someday I hope to have a pump installed so we can have a fountain or a water feature in it.

A few weeks ago, I was working and happened to walk to the window just as a flash of blue and white caught my eye, coming around the far side of the building. I have been working with these young men long enough to know that someone was making a run for it. This was a fairly typical occurrence: one of the boys would get angry or frustrated, and their gut reaction would be to run. They had not yet learned how to step up and face their problems; they had always simply avoided them. This behavior had been modeled at home since they were young kids. Fight or flight: these were the typical responses to conflict and difficulty.

And this young man chose flight. I wasn't too worried he was going to run away. It was close to half a mile to the entrance of Chestnut Mountain Ranch and then probably another half mile up a long hill to get to a road of any size. They usually collapsed in a heaving heap of sweat and gasps before they were out of sight.

I am not sure if this particular young man had been a runner before, but regardless, he had a different approach to his "escape" that I had not yet, or since, seen duplicated. Most likely because it was about the worst escape attempt ever.

As he rounded the building, I noticed he took a little sharper turn than he would need to if he planned to make it down the road. Instead he lined his path up with the pond, and after a few steps it became apparent what he had in mind. I am not sure if I smiled outwardly, but inside my heart warmed just a little, and I raised my coffee mug to take a sip and enjoy what I was pretty sure was about to happen.

Sure enough, he sighted in on that little pond and kicked it into high gear. Five steps from the edge of the water, I could see his eyes widen, then narrow with focus and determination. The look on his face told me, in his mind, he thought this was going to be epic. I had to agree.

Two more steps and he gathered himself for a launch, his arms slowly coming behind him in ready position to hurl himself into the atmosphere. Unfortunately for him, the ground was a bit uneven, and at his great speed, a rock caught his foot and caused him to stumble. His next-to-last step caught a tuft of grass, and with a look of combined terror and sheer determination he was able to get his foot enough underneath his body to manage a final, heroic push.

It was not the prettiest jump I have ever seen, not by a long shot, and the landing wasn't much better. His momentum carried him forward in an ungraceful arc right into the dirty brown water of the retaining pond; it was more of a face flop than anything else. Honestly, it looked like it hurt, and I think I heard every joint in his back crack.

The splash was formidable, and as I watched the muddy brown water explode up into the air and then fall back to earth enveloping his body. I said a short prayer of thanks to our heavenly Father for calling me to work with troubled boys. Some days, my heart overflows.

What that day's runner did not realize is that drainage ponds typically have anywhere from a foot to 18 inches of mud silt settled on the bottom. This is very messy and unyielding mud. It'll stop a truck with no problem.

As the water settled, all I could see was the crown of his head sticking ever so slightly above the waterline. I leaned forward and looked a bit closer after he didn't move for a couple seconds; I thought he may have spiked himself to the bottom of the pond, but after a brief moment he slowly stood up, head slightly bowed, covered in black muck, and probably wondering why that hadn't gone better.

He turned and looked up at my office. Maybe he sensed me looking at him. Our eyes met, and I raised my mug in tribute.

Having been focused on our young hero, I didn't notice that Clay, our program director and a good friend from our Eagle Ranch days, had emerged from around the corner. He was standing about 20 feet away, taking in the same scene as I was. His hands were in his pockets as he waited for the young man to extract himself from the mud. As he did, Clay sat down on a small set of steps and motioned for the boy to join him so they could talk for a minute. Clay is a very kind and patient man.

Pretty defeated, very muddy, and soaking wet, the young man sloshed his way to the steps and sat down. I couldn't hear them from where I stood, but they must have talked for a half hour at least. Eventually I saw them stand, and side by side, slowly walk back around the same corner from which they had come.

I tell you this story because when you work with troubled boys, these kinds of things happen all the time. Well, not exactly like this. This was pretty fantastic. But much of the work we do is on the steps of a home or building after some upset teen has thrown himself in a drainage pond, metaphorically speaking.

It is anonymous, unglamorous, and difficult work. Our staff understands that the work they do is not about them; it is about the boys and their families who come to us being restored. This is perspective.

It would be hard to say how many hours our staff, clearly out of the public eye, are ministering to these kids. In fact, they are doing the real work, quietly and behind closed doors. There are not too many people who sign up for that kind of job. I am lucky to have some of the most kind, caring, and selfless people on the planet on staff. We wouldn't be what we are today without their tireless efforts.

In my role, I am the face of Chestnut Mountain Ranch. I get many of the speaking engagements and public recognition for the work we are doing. I have to watch my motives to make sure I am not leading only to be noticed or admired as someone who has done something big and important in the world. Good leaders do not build their organizations and ministries so people will look up to and marvel at them.

In some ways, our expectation (probably subconsciously) is that we should be rewarded or acknowledge sooner rather than later for the good we do. For those of us who lead, it can be tempting to get accustomed to the praise and adoration of people who follow and support the ministry God has given to us. It is like a drug and can be hard to resist when it comes.

Alternately, when the praise is lacking, we start to wonder and doubt: What is going on? Where are the followers, the congratulations, the praise?

God's perspective reminds us it is not only OK to labor in secret—like Clay and that boy, just the two of them on a back porch in the middle of hundreds of acres of woods—it is actually preferable. That may sound a bit crazy, but I think Jesus gives us a little insight into how God operates in Matthew's Gospel:

> *So when you give to the needy, do not announce it with trumpets, as the hypocrites do in the synagogues and on the streets, to be honored by others. Truly I tell you, they have received their reward in full. But when you give to the needy, do not let your left hand know what your right hand is doing, so that your giving may be in secret. Then your Father, who sees what is done in secret, will reward you.*
>
> *—Matthew 6:2-4*

There is something extremely counterintuitive here, especially for those in ministry. Our natural inclination is to shout our achievements and accomplishments from the rooftops. I think this is maybe because there is a very real competition for dollars among most churches and nonprofits, and people like to give to "effective" ministries. But the biblical principle is to give in secret. I understand there is a balance here, with being open with donors. I think it is safe to say 90 percent or more of all the work our staff does is done in secret, without public acknowledgement.

But here's the thing: the Father sees. And He will reward. For me, that is a pretty intriguing idea. Who would you rather get your praise from? A bunch of civilians or the Creator? Yeah, I thought so. Me too.

We don't need, nor should we even desire, the credit. If that's why you're getting into ministry, as some sort of ego boost, then your perspective is way off.

But we don't have to worry because we know God is good on His promises, and He promises our labor and work will not go unnoticed. He sees, and He will reward you.

And I think that is pretty exciting.

In 1 Thessalonians 2, Paul goes on and on about how much he cared for the Thessalonians, like a father and mother (talk about thankless jobs!), and how deep his affection was for them. He reminds them how he had labored on their behalf and expected nothing in return and how he was happy to do so because of his great love for them. And then he says something that shows his perspective on all his work, the reason for the difficult journeys he took to share the gospel of Jesus with them and many others, the beatings and imprisonment he endured, the humiliation and brushes with death. He writes this:

> For what is our hope, our joy, or the crown in which we will glory in the presence of our Lord Jesus when he comes? Is it not you? Indeed, you are our glory and joy.
> —1 Thessalonians 2:19–20

I don't always have this perspective. I don't always remember that God will one day reward the efforts of those who labor for His sake with great joy and glory, and the reward will be the people we love and strive to serve.

And I think that is going to be a very good day.

AFTERWORD

While this has primarily been a book about having the right set of values and skills in place, a lot more still needs to be done to see the seed God has planted in you come to fruition. More "nuts and bolts" type things. And so I wanted to provide a short checklist for practical steps to starting a ministry:

WRITE A VISION STATEMENT

A vision statement is a short, concise message that captures the essence of what you want to do and accomplish. A vision statement clearly states the main goal and purpose of your organization. And here's a hint: the shorter the better because it will be more focused and more memorable for others learning about what you do. Our vision at Chestnut Mountain Ranch is to provide a Christ-centered school and home for boys in crisis and in need of hope and healing. Partnering with their families, we pursue family restoration and reunification.

DEFINE YOUR VALUES

Values are the things that matter the most to you, and they are vital for any organization because they help guide in the decision-making process. For example, we decided early on we would be debt-free in building Chestnut Mountain Ranch. And that value kept us from taking a loan to build the ranch and protected us from some financial peril. Some of our other values include: God and His Word, people, excellence, and authenticity. People will know and relate to your organization based upon what you value, so this is an important step in the process and something that should be established early.

WRITE A BUSINESS PLAN

Although time consuming and sometimes tedious for those new at the process, a well-written business plan will help tremendously in the long run to get your vision off the ground. Thinking through and writing about your business will force you to consider both the need for what you are doing in your area and how you are going to pull it off. It is a tremendously practical document that includes:

> *A needs assessment or market analysis:* This section helps you understand the needs for your organization and what you are going to do. Also, you will need to research and see what other similar groups are doing, if they are doing it the same as you want to, or differently, and if so, how? As we were looking to start Chestnut Mountain Ranch, we discovered West Virginia has a huge high school dropout, pregnancy, and drug-use rate for young people and very few agencies helping.

> *A business model:* This section explains how you are going to operate. What are your processes to meet the need in your area? At Chestnut Mountain Ranch we start with education at our school and then incorporate individual and family counseling and then, finally, the residency program. An alternate approach might be to operate as a counseling center that includes education.

> *An organizational structure:* What will the organization look like in terms of structure? What roles will there be in the program, finances, facilities, communication, etc.? This will give you a sense of what roles and responsibilities you will need to fill. At Chestnut Mountain Ranch, we have communication, education, counseling,

residency, and facilities departments, all with their own unique responsibilities.

A five-year budget: This can be a difficult task with no history and experience to inform your estimates, but it is an extremely helpful process and will give you some sense of the realities of starting an organization. These targets will also help you ascertain your fundraising goals.

Key milestones: Milestones, or key goals, are basically a sequential to-do list and will keep you on track to see your vision become a reality. The steps I am taking you through in this afterword could be the basic milestones for your organization.

BUILD YOUR CORE TEAM

There is no doubt you are going to want and need people to help build your organization. Although building a team is an ongoing progress, it is especially critical in the early stages to work with people who share your vision and values. I suggest starting with four to five people you trust who have experience in business or ministry, and invite them to be on your board of directors. They will be an invaluable resource as you get started.

BUILD YOUR PLATFORM

Your platform is those people who will listen to you about your vision and organization. Depending on what you are doing they may include individuals, families, churches, businesses, or other organizations. You will need people to support and finance your vision, so this is a key process. Steps include: developing a presentation and website (and perhaps print materials) based on your vision, values, and business plan, brainstorming a list of potential contacts, and picking up the phone to schedule meetings and appointments.

BUILD THE ORGANIZATION

Finally, you will need to start building the actual organization, the mechanism that will do what you have in your heart to do. This will be different for everyone, but some key organizational components to consider are:

Establish the legal structure: What needs to be in place, including federal, state, county, and local licenses? Applying for and obtaining 501(c)3 status with the federal government is probably a good idea in most cases, as it gives an added incentive for people to support your ministry. It may be a good idea to consult with an attorney early on to be sure the necessary legal structure is in place. Liability insurance is important and could be discussed with your lawyer and an insurance agent.

Determine your financial process: It is vital to clearly established processes for tracking and accounting all donations and expenditures. It is probably worth the money to hire an accountant to help get set up and define protocol for you, as it will save you headaches down the road and increase donor confidence that their gifts are being well-stewarded.

Set up your facilities and offices: Depending on your vision and milestones, you will need to establish a "home base" for your organization. Office space, phones, computers, etc. will all need to be considered and included in the budget. A local real estate agent may be very helpful in finding and negotiating a location for your organization.

Consider staffing needs: It is a big step to begin hiring for your organization (one that brings a whole host of considerations, such as benefits, taxes, insurance, etc.), and you should take the time to consider what positions are most vital for each phase of development. For example, a communications director may be most vital in the beginning to help spread the word and build the platform, while a facilities director can wait until later, when there are actual facilities to direct. You should prioritize key staff positions and develop job descriptions for each. Your personal network may be the best place for recruiting staff or engage the services of a local staffing agency.

Begin operation: Keeping your milestones in mind, start your organization's operations one phase at a time. For example, at Chestnut Mountain Ranch, although we knew we would be a residential school eventually, we started with a day school first, which gave us some new momentum in raising money for the boys' homes. And right now our school is housed in the bottom floor of our administration building but will eventually be moved to its own building.

This is not an exhaustive checklist by any stretch of the imagination, but hopefully it provides you with a rough framework to start. And sometimes that is all it takes, the courage to follow God's leading in your life and to start. And we pray that God will bless your efforts and obedience to follow Him.

ABOUT CHESTNUT MOUNTAIN RANCH

I am from West Virginia but moved to Georgia when I was young, after my father passed. I grew up in Atlanta, and when I was 21 years old, I became a police officer. For 11 years I worked as a Christian in uniform. I loved my work, but God began to stir my wife's heart and mine for something more. A few years later we left our careers and became houseparents in one of the boys' homes at Eagle Ranch, just north of Atlanta. We committed to three years there, and during that time we saw a ministry program that worked. Lives were being changed. Families restored. Young men were coming to know Christ in a real way. The vision grew. We felt God calling us to replicate this ministry in a state where the need was the highest. We conducted state by state research, developed business plans, and prayed for over a year before even speaking of this to anyone.

Everything pointed to West Virginia. Back in 2004, my wife (Dawn) and I started speaking to others about the vision of Chestnut Mountain Ranch. We were living and working at Eagle Ranch in Georgia at the time. Eagle Ranch staff helped us prepare for this journey we were about to set out on. The preparation was key. The vision was made clear, the plan checked by many, and after much prayer we moved to West Virginia with the hope that God would make His presence known in the vision and help build the place of hope and healing

Since landing here, we essentially burned our ships and hunkered down to see this through. Many storms have come, and fundraising in West Virginia in the middle of tough national economic times has been nothing short of challenging.

I am proud to tell you that we have started taking in our first boys! We started with the day program utilizing the ranch school. Our phones are ringing for additional children.

Having the first group of boys here has been special. We have a great group of young men, and we have more enrolling this summer. The past several weeks have been a sweet season of life for me, my family, the ranch staff, board members, volunteers, and the families and boys that are being helped through the ranch program, We have all worked hard to see this day come.

Many of the boys applying for the ranch live too far away for the families to be able to drive in each day. We need to get the homes up so we can begin helping these families. The homes will enable us to provide a safe place for the boys to experience a healthy home and be able to remain at the ranch throughout the week while attending school.

After seven years of preparing, we are witnessing the fruit of our labor. I welcome you to come and meet the boys and the staff, and see firsthand what you have invested in.

OUR VISION

Chestnut Mountain Ranch will establish an academic environment to motivate the student to use his gifts and abilities for God's glory (Proverbs 22:6). Consistent encouragement, meaningful relationships, and quality instruction will help the student and his family realize God's purpose in every aspect of their lives and equip them to make sound choices.

Chestnut Mountain Ranch is located just six miles south of Morgantown, West Virginia, on 225 beautiful acres. The ranch is a Christ-centered safe haven for boys and families in crisis . . . a place for family restoration, where boys can enjoy school again, and all can experience positive family values.

We modeled Chestnut Mountain Ranch after the 25-plus year program called Eagle Ranch. Located in Georgia, Eagle Ranch is nationally recognized as one of the best programs in the country, and has been featured on notable programs such as CNN News.

SCHOOL BELIEFS

These are the beliefs that help to guide the staff in our efforts to help the boys, and their families, experience the wonderful things God is able to do in our lives. We believe:

- Every student is constantly learning.

- Every word and action of the teacher needs to speak godliness into the student's life.

- As the student develops a relationship with Jesus, God's transforming power molds his character enabling him to become God's image bearer (intellectually, morally, relationally, and emotionally).

- The student needs to be trained to properly represent God as His image bearer.

- Every student learns best in a relational, tutorial approach where curriculum and environment are tailored to meet his individual needs.

- Healthy relationships with adults are vital to a student's academic, physical, and spiritual development.

- The student is able to learn from the natural consequences of his decisions in a well-structured, consistent, safe, and supportive environment.

OUR SCRIPTURAL FOCUS

You were taught, with regard to your former way of life, to put off your old self, which is being corrupted by its deceitful desires; to be made new in the attitude of your minds.
—Ephesians 4:22–23

Therefore, if anyone is in Christ, the new creation has come: The old has gone, the new is here!
—2 Corinthians 5:17

Visit ChestnutMountainRanch.org to learn more about the ministry of Chestnut Mountain Ranch.

Give a GIFT OF HOPE

ᴛʜᴇ "Gɪꜰᴛs ᴏꜰ Hᴏᴘᴇ" ꜱᴇʀɪᴇꜱ offers hope to those walking through some of life's ost challenging circumstances. Each book offers 30 devotionals, Scripture, and ayers that provide readers inspiration and encouragement.

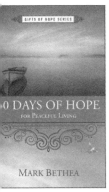

30 DAYS OF HOPE
ꜰᴏʀ Pᴇᴀᴄᴇꜰᴜʟ Lɪᴠɪɴɢ

MARK BETHEA

N154115
$9.99 plus s&h

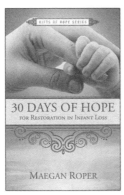

30 DAYS OF HOPE
ꜰᴏʀ Rᴇꜱᴛᴏʀᴀᴛɪᴏɴ ɪɴ Iɴꜰᴀɴᴛ Lᴏꜱꜱ

MAEGAN ROPER

N154116
$9.99 plus s&h

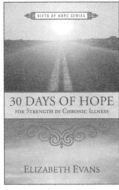

30 DAYS OF HOPE
ꜰᴏʀ Sᴛʀᴇɴɢᴛʜ ɪɴ Cʜʀᴏɴɪᴄ Iʟʟɴᴇꜱꜱ

ELIZABETH EVANS

N164105
$9.99 plus s&h

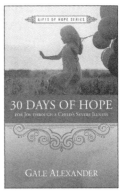

30 DAYS OF HOPE
ꜰᴏʀ Jᴏʏ ᴛʜʀᴏᴜɢʜ ᴀ Cʜɪʟᴅ'ꜱ Sᴇᴠᴇʀᴇ Iʟʟɴᴇꜱꜱ

GALE ALEXANDER

N164115
$9.99 plus s&h

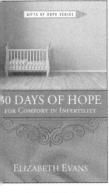

30 DAYS OF HOPE
ꜰᴏʀ Cᴏᴍꜰᴏʀᴛ ɪɴ Iɴꜰᴇʀᴛɪʟɪᴛʏ

ELIZABETH EVANS

N164104
$9.99 plus s&h

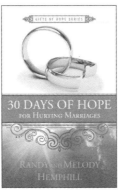

30 DAYS OF HOPE
ꜰᴏʀ Hᴜʀᴛɪɴɢ Mᴀʀʀɪᴀɢᴇꜱ

RANDY ᴀɴᴅ MELODY HEMPHILL

N174106
$9.99 plus s&h

30 DAYS OF HOPE
ꜰᴏʀ Aᴅᴏᴘᴛɪᴠᴇ Pᴀʀᴇɴᴛꜱ

JENNIFER PHILLIPS

N174113
$9.99 plus s&h

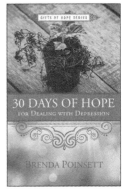

30 DAYS OF HOPE
ꜰᴏʀ Dᴇᴀʟɪɴɢ ᴡɪᴛʜ Dᴇᴘʀᴇꜱꜱɪᴏɴ

BRENDA POINSETT

N174118
$9.99 plus s&h
Coming June 2017!

ᐯisit **NewHopePublishers.com** to learn more about the "Gifts of Hope" series, read sample chapters, and more.